TEAM

Welcome to "Napoleon: The Conqueror" - a thorough exploration into the life, ambition, genius, and downfall of one of history's most enigmatic figures, Napoleon Bonaparte. Crafted meticulously by the ChatStick Team, this biography sheds new light on the intricate dynamics that led to the rise and fall of a man whose very name embodies power, conquest, and transformation.

Engross yourself in this epic narrative that travels through time, from the humble beginnings of Napoleon's childhood in Corsica to his astounding ascendance as Emperor of the French. Unravel the complexities of his leadership, ambition, and the strategic acumen that both established and, eventually, dismantled his empire. Every page of this book promises to imbue readers with profound insights into the man behind the legend and the circumstances that shaped his monumental life.

chatvariety.com

table of contents

01
Introduction

02
Childhood and Early Life

03
Early Military Career

04
The Italian Campaign

05
The Egyptian Campaign and the Rise to Power

06
Napoleon as First Consul

chatvariety.com

table of contents

07
Napoleon as Emperor

08
The Grand Empire and the Continental System

09
Downfall: The Invasion of Russia

10
Exile, Return, and Final Defeat

11
Legacy and Conclusion

chatvariety.com

INTRODUCTION

Chapter 01: A Brief Overview of Napoleon Bonaparte

Who is Napoleon Bonaparte? A question so simple yet so complex that it has captured the imagination of historians, scholars, and history enthusiasts for more than two centuries. There are many ways to approach this query - through his myriad titles: a French statesman, a military leader, an Emperor; through his achievements and failures, his character traits, or his enduring legacy that still affects us today. However, this book's purpose goes beyond just understanding Napoleon Bonaparte. It's about getting to know him in all his brilliance, ambition, and contradiction - an exercise that requires us to delve deeper, to peel back the layers of history and uncover the man beneath the myth.

Napoleon Bonaparte was a man of remarkable ability and ambition. Born in 1769 to an impoverished noble family on the island of Corsica, he rose to prominence amidst the chaotic backdrop of the French Revolution. He quickly proved himself as a military leader of unparalleled strategic acumen, leading his troops to victory in numerous campaigns across Europe and beyond. His name soon became synonymous with victory, as his genius on the battlefield seemed to know no bounds.

However, Napoleon wasn't just a military leader. In 1799, he seized political power in France in a coup d'état and in 1804 declared himself Emperor. As a ruler, he implemented a wide array of political and social reforms that brought stability and modernity to France. His laws, collectively known as the Napoleonic Code, would profoundly shape many nations' legal systems.

Napoleon was an audacious character whose ambition knew no limits. He dreamed of a unified Europe under French rule, and for a time, it seemed like he would achieve that vision. At the height of his power, Napoleon controlled vast swaths of the continent. But this period, known as the Napoleonic Wars, was also marked by relentless conflict, as Napoleon's expansionist ambitions brought him into collision with virtually every major European power.

Like Icarus flying too close to the sun, Napoleon's thirst for power would eventually lead to his downfall. After a disastrous campaign in Russia and his defeat at the Battle of Waterloo, Napoleon was exiled twice, finally ending his days on the remote island of Saint Helena. But even in defeat and death, Napoleon left an indelible mark on the world. His rise and fall stand as one of history's most dramatic sagas, a tale of ambition, genius, and hubris in equal measure.

So, this book is an invitation - an invitation to step back in time and walk in Napoleon's footsteps. To explore his life and times, to understand his thoughts and actions, and to appreciate his impact on our world. This journey is not just about Napoleon Bonaparte, the larger-than-life historical figure. It's about Napoleon the man - his dreams, his fears, his strengths, his weaknesses. It's about understanding what drove him, what he achieved, and what he lost.

In the following chapters, we will delve into every aspect of Napoleon's life, from his childhood and early military career, his momentous rise to power, his transformative rule as Emperor, and his eventual downfall and exile. We will also reflect on his enduring legacy and the lessons his life offers us today.

This is the story of Napoleon Bonaparte - a man who embodied the contradictions of his age, a man who reached for the stars only to fall from the sky. It's a complex, captivating, and ultimately human story. And it's a story that we hope will enrich your understanding and appreciation of this extraordinary individual who continues to cast a long shadow over our world. Welcome to "Napoleon: The Conqueror."

Chapter 02: The significance of his role in European

As we begin our journey through the extraordinary life of Napoleon Bonaparte, it's essential to place him within the broader context of European history. Napoleon was not just a man of his time; he was a man who shaped his time. His influence reverberated far beyond the borders of his French Empire and continues to be felt to this day. Napoleon's impact on European history is so profound that it's nearly impossible to study the era without devoting substantial attention to his role.

When Napoleon rose to prominence, Europe was in a state of flux. The French Revolution had not only upended the French monarchy but also sent shockwaves across a continent where monarchies were the norm. The revolutionary ideas of liberty, equality, and fraternity were challenging centuries-old traditions and hierarchies.

Amid this chaos, Napoleon emerged as a stabilizing force. His military genius helped France defend the Revolution against various European powers intent on restoring the monarchy. As the leader of France, first as First Consul and then as Emperor, Napoleon gave the nation a sense of direction that it lacked in the tumultuous years following the Revolution. He consolidated the gains of the Revolution while tempering its excesses.

Under his leadership, France underwent comprehensive reforms that transformed every aspect of French society. The Napoleonic Code, for instance, has had a lasting impact, not only on France but on many other nations around the world. His sweeping modernizations of administration, education, and law have shaped France and other parts of Europe in ways that are still evident today.

On a broader scale, Napoleon reshaped the map of Europe. Through his numerous military campaigns, he toppled monarchies, redrew borders, and spread the ideas of the French Revolution across the continent. His ambitious vision for a unified Europe under French influence was a forerunner to the modern European Union concept.

However, Napoleon's rule was also a period of constant warfare. His aggressive expansionist policies led to the Napoleonic Wars, which caused immense suffering and loss of life. These wars changed the face of warfare and set the stage for the conflicts of the 19th and 20th centuries.

Napoleon's eventual downfall had significant repercussions for Europe. His defeat led to the Congress of Vienna's restoration of balance among European powers, shaping the continent's political landscape for the next century. The fall of Napoleon also marked the end of the French Revolution era, ushering in a period of relative peace in Europe.

As we delve deeper into Napoleon's life in the following chapters, we'll discover a man of immense ambition, stunning genius, and glaring flaws. We'll see how he rose from obscurity to rule a vast empire, how he changed France and Europe, and how his overreach led to his downfall.

Napoleon's story is not just one man's tale. It's the story of a period in history that saw a seismic shift in political, social, and cultural norms. It's the story of Europe at the turn of a new era, with Napoleon at its helm. By understanding Napoleon, we gain insight into this transformative period in European history.

So, as we embark on this journey through the life of Napoleon Bonaparte, remember that we're not just exploring the life of an extraordinary individual. We're also uncovering the story of a continent in the throes of change, a story in which Napoleon played a leading role. Welcome to Chapter 2 of "Napoleon: The Conqueror."

Chapter 03: The Objectives and Scope of the Book

In this chapter, we turn our attention towards the objectives and the scope of our exploration into the life and times of Napoleon Bonaparte, the central figure in our book, "Napoleon: The Conqueror."

The primary objective of this book is to provide a detailed and nuanced portrait of Napoleon Bonaparte, one of history's most influential figures. We aim to delve into the depths of his life, from his humble beginnings on the island of Corsica to his rise as one of the world's most powerful leaders, and finally, his eventual downfall. We aspire to paint a holistic picture, looking not only at his military and political prowess but also at the man behind the public figure - his personal life, his relationships, his thoughts, and his aspirations.

Our exploration is not limited to the narrative of his life. We will also examine the broader context of the time in which Napoleon lived, shedding light on the turbulent era that both shaped him and was, in turn, shaped by him. Our journey will traverse through the French Revolution, the Napoleonic Wars, and the significant social, political, and cultural changes that marked this period in history.

One of the key goals of this book is to unravel the complexities of Napoleon's character. Was he a liberator who spread the ideals of the French Revolution or a tyrant bent on personal aggrandizement? Was he a military genius or a reckless conqueror whose ambition brought about his own ruin? Through an in-depth examination of his actions and decisions, we aim to provide the reader with the necessary context and analysis to form their own interpretations.

Furthermore, we will examine the lasting impact Napoleon had on France, Europe, and indeed the world. His legacy persists in various forms - from the codes of law he established to the political landscape he shaped. By understanding Napoleon's influence, we can better comprehend the world as we know it today.

This book is intended for a broad audience. Whether you are a student looking for comprehensive information for your research, a history enthusiast wanting to delve deeper into the Napoleonic era, or a casual reader interested in the life of this fascinating individual, "Napoleon: The Conqueror" is for you.

Our approach is to be detailed yet accessible. We've endeavored to ensure that complex ideas and historical events are explained in a manner that is easy to understand without compromising on academic rigour. While we explore the depths of Napoleon's life, our tone remains friendly and engaging, ensuring a pleasant reading experience.

Finally, we aim to spark a conversation. This book is not just about providing information but also about promoting thought and discourse. We invite you to question, to debate, and to ponder as you join us on this captivating journey through one of history's most interesting periods.

With these objectives and scope in mind, we invite you to delve into the pages of "Napoleon: The Conqueror," an in-depth study of Napoleon's ambition, genius, and downfall. Let's embark on this fascinating journey together, as we uncover the life and legacy of Napoleon Bonaparte.

CHILDHOOD AND EARLY LIFE

chapter 04
Birthplace and Family Background

Napoleon Bonaparte, the man who would later command armies, shape nations, and influence the course of European history, began his life in a place far removed from the glamour of palaces and the clamour of battlefields. The narrative of his childhood offers a glimpse into his early years and the circumstances that would help mould him into the man he was to become.

Born on August 15, 1769, in the vibrant town of Ajaccio, on the western coast of Corsica, Napoleon's early life was framed by the beauty of the Mediterranean and the rugged landscapes of the island. His birthplace, a modest stone house, was no palace, but it was a nurturing environment for the young Napoleon.

Corsica itself had an atmosphere of fervent nationalism and resistance against foreign dominance. Only a year before Napoleon's birth, the island had been sold to France by the Republic of Genoa. This left a deep imprint on the Corsican people, who were fiercely proud of their culture and heritage. This spirit of defiance against oppression would later echo in Napoleon's own life and ambition.

Napoleon was born into the minor nobility of Corsica. The Bonaparte family was of Italian origin, with ancestry tracing back to Tuscan nobility. His father, Carlo Maria di Buonaparte, was an attorney who represented Corsica at the court of the French King. He was a man of intellect and integrity, who had a profound influence on his son.

His mother, Letizia Ramolino, was known for her beauty and resilience. It was from her that Napoleon inherited his indomitable will and tenacity. Despite the hardships of raising eight children (Napoleon was the second) in an often tumultuous environment, Letizia was a pillar of strength for her family.

The Bonaparte household was a dynamic one, teeming with life, debates, and a shared sense of Corsican pride. It was in this home, among his siblings, Joseph, Lucien, Elisa, Louis, Pauline, Caroline, and Jerome, that Napoleon spent his formative years. Their relationships varied from deeply supportive to profoundly competitive, influencing Napoleon's outlook and character in more ways than one.

Napoleon's early education was primarily at home, with the help of tutors. A pivotal change came when, at the age of nine, he was sent to the mainland to attend school in Autun and later, the military academy in Brienne. This was his first real interaction with French culture and his initial step towards the larger world beyond Corsica.

Looking back, Napoleon's childhood was filled with paradoxes. On the one hand, there was the simple, rugged life in Corsica; on the other, the promise of nobility and opportunities that lay ahead. This interplay of contrast and harmony, struggle and opportunity, was the cradle that nurtured the child who would grow up to be Napoleon Bonaparte, the Conqueror.

In the next chapters, we'll delve deeper into Napoleon's educational journey, his military career, and his rapid ascent to power. We'll witness the raw material of his childhood honed into the sharp blade of ambition, leadership, and genius. But for now, we leave the young Napoleon at the cusp of his life's great adventure, staring wide-eyed at the vast mainland that would soon know his name.

Chapter 05: The Influences during Childhood

Napoleon Bonaparte once said, "The future destiny of the child is always the work of the mother." As we delve deeper into Napoleon's early life, it becomes clear how profound this statement is. His childhood was studded with experiences and influences that helped shape his character, ambition, and approach to life.

To begin, we must return to Napoleon's mother, Letizia Ramolino. Letizia, despite her genteel background, was a woman of robust strength and determination. She raised her children with a firm hand, instilling in them a strong sense of discipline and responsibility from a young age. Her influence on Napoleon was particularly pronounced. He often referred to her as his guide, a beacon that helped him navigate the tumultuous seas of his life.

Letizia's influence extended beyond just discipline and determination. She was a woman deeply connected to her Corsican roots, and her passion for her homeland was infectious. This fierce sense of loyalty and nationalism is an element that Napoleon would carry throughout his life, reflected in his commitment to France.

Napoleon's father, Carlo Maria di Buonaparte, was also a significant influence, but in a different way. Carlo was a man of intellect, an attorney, and a diplomat who held progressive views. He was one of the few Corsican nobles who advocated cooperation with French rule, believing that it was the best way for Corsica and its people to prosper. It was from Carlo that Napoleon inherited his knack for diplomacy and political strategy.

The island of Corsica itself was an enormous influence on Napoleon. With its rugged landscapes and the proud spirit of its people, it was a world in its own right, remote from the glitz and politics of mainland Europe. Living here during his formative years, Napoleon learned the importance of resilience and self-reliance. The island's turbulent history of resisting foreign rule also had a profound impact on him, fostering in him a deep disdain for any form of oppression.

Napoleon's siblings also played a crucial role in shaping his character. The Bonaparte household was a vibrant hive of personalities, ideas, and ambitions. Joseph, his elder brother, was someone Napoleon looked up to, whereas his younger siblings provided him an opportunity to practice leadership. The competition and camaraderie amongst the siblings often reflected in Napoleon's later interactions with his military comrades and political allies.

His early education, first with tutors in Corsica, and later in schools in mainland France, also had a profound impact on young Napoleon. The strict discipline and rigorous academic environment of these institutions introduced him to the wider world of knowledge, shaping his intellectual curiosity and critical thinking skills.

In summary, Napoleon's childhood was a crucible of experiences and influences. From his parents, he learned the values of determination, discipline, and strategy. His birthplace instilled in him a sense of resilience, love for his homeland, and a rebellious spirit against oppression. His siblings offered him a field to practice leadership, and his schooling molded his intellectual abilities.

Every one of these influences played a part in creating the man who would later conquer Europe. In the chapters that follow, we will see how these childhood lessons, imbibed early and carried forward into his adult life, informed Napoleon's journey from being an ambitious young man to becoming a powerful emperor. It is indeed a fascinating tale, so let's continue with the story, my dear reader.

Chapter 06: Brienne and Paris Military School

Welcome back, dear reader! We continue our journey through Napoleon's early life by focusing on the next stage: his education. We explore the learning institutions that shaped Napoleon Bonaparte into the man of iron will and strategic genius, starting from the sleepy town of Brienne-le-Château to the bustling city of Paris.

The story starts in 1779 when a young Napoleon, barely ten years old, left his beloved Corsica for the first time to attend the Royal Military School in Brienne, located in northeastern France. The transition from the Mediterranean island's rustic charm to the strict discipline of the French school was a dramatic one for the young Napoleon.

Brienne was not just a school; it was a completely new universe for Napoleon. Here, sons of noblemen from across France received a rigorous education, preparing them for service in the army or the church. The school fostered a fiercely competitive environment that steeled Napoleon's resolve, pushing him to overcome challenges, even those as trivial as learning French, a language he initially struggled with.

In Brienne, Napoleon's intellectual brilliance began to shine. He had a penchant for history and geography, often spending hours immersed in tales of great conquerors and intricate maps of far-off lands. His teachers noted his exceptional ability to recall facts and dates, his analytical mind dissecting the success and failures of historical figures. Such were the early signs of the military strategist he would one day become.

Napoleon's time at Brienne was also marked by his solitude. He was often ostracized by his peers for his Corsican accent and his less-than-aristocratic lineage. While it might have been painful, this experience developed in him a resilience and an independent spirit that would later become his trademarks.

After completing five years at Brienne, Napoleon earned a scholarship to the prestigious École Militaire in Paris, the premier military academy in France. At the age of 15, he was one of the youngest in his class, but what he lacked in age, he made up in determination and intellect.

At École Militaire, Napoleon's education took on a more specialized focus. He studied artillery tactics and mathematics, areas that fascinated him and would become key tools in his military arsenal. He graduated a year early, at the age of 16, due to the sudden death of his father, which put his family in a financial strain. Despite this personal tragedy, Napoleon had made his mark at École Militaire, finishing his course as a second lieutenant - a significant accomplishment for someone of his age.

His years at Brienne and École Militaire were transformative for Napoleon. They presented him with challenges that tested his mettle and revealed his potential. These institutions also provided him with the foundational knowledge and skills that would guide his future military strategies.

Dear reader, as we close this chapter on Napoleon's early education, we can see the outline of the extraordinary man he was to become. The tenacious child from Corsica was slowly, but surely, transforming into a formidable strategist and leader. As we move forward, let's delve into how these early experiences shaped his initial steps in his illustrious military career. The story is only getting more exciting, so please, stay with us!

EARLY MILITARY CAREER

Chapter 07: Role in the French Revolution

Hello again, dear reader! Our narrative now takes us to the cusp of one of the most tumultuous periods in French history - the French Revolution - and our protagonist, the young Napoleon, is right in the thick of it. Let's delve into how these events further shaped the ambitious Corsican's path to greatness.

In 1789, as the French Revolution erupted, Napoleon was stationed in Paris. He was a young and ambitious artillery officer, keenly observing the historic shift occurring around him. His initial years in the military had exposed him to the endemic corruption and inefficiencies within the French military structure. He saw the Revolution as a necessary purge, a way to rid France of its entrenched societal and political ills.

Napoleon, who had always been passionate about social and political equity, found himself naturally aligning with the principles of the Revolution. He quickly embraced the ideals of liberty, equality, and fraternity. Despite his noble status, he felt a deep connection with the common man's struggle against the oppressive Ancien Régime, which perhaps stemmed from his own experiences of alienation during his education.

The Revolution gave Napoleon an opportunity to shine. His first major assignment was to quell a royalist uprising threatening the revolutionary government in Paris in 1795, known as the 13 Vendémiaire. Napoleon strategically employed his artillery forces to disperse the royalist forces, demonstrating his tactical prowess and decisive leadership. His swift success earned him recognition and the appointment as commander of the French Army of the Interior.

However, Napoleon was not just a military man in the midst of a political revolution. He was also a thinker, regularly attending meetings of the Jacobin Club, a radical political group. He wrote and published political and philosophical tracts, his 'Le Souper de Beaucaire' standing out for its discussion of how the Revolution could unite France rather than tear it apart.

It's also important to note that during the Revolution, Napoleon met key individuals who would become instrumental in his future. Among them were Paul Barras, a powerful politician who became Napoleon's patron, and Joséphine de Beauharnais, who would later become his first wife and Empress.

The French Revolution, despite its tumult and violence, served as the ideal backdrop for Napoleon's advancement. The old hierarchical constraints had been swept away, creating opportunities for talented and ambitious individuals like him to rise through the ranks.

In the end, dear reader, the Revolution provided Napoleon with the stage on which he could demonstrate his military acumen, political savvy, and his commitment to revolutionary ideals. These factors would significantly contribute to his rise to power, which we will explore in the chapters to come. The narrative of Napoleon is as exciting as it is intricate, so please, stick around for more!

Chapter 08: Rise in the French Military

Hello again, dear reader, let's continue our journey through the life of Napoleon Bonaparte! In this chapter, we delve into the rapid rise of Napoleon in the French military, an ascent facilitated by his early achievements and innate tactical genius.

In the aftermath of the French Revolution, Napoleon found himself at the helm of the Army of the Interior, an appointment he owed to his successful quelling of the royalist uprising in 1795. He was just 26, an age when most are beginning their careers, yet Napoleon was already commanding a major French army.

In 1796, he received his first independent command, the French Army of Italy. His performance in this campaign would mark his arrival on the world stage as a military genius. The Italian campaign was nothing short of miraculous. Despite leading an under-supplied and demoralized army, Napoleon managed to defeat the Austrian and Piedmontese forces through a series of swift and audacious maneuvers. His innovative strategies, focusing on speed, aggression, and the element of surprise, brought France victory after victory, most notably at the battles of Lodi, Arcole, and Rivoli.

Napoleon's personal charisma played a crucial role in these victories. He had an uncanny ability to inspire his troops, often leading from the front and sharing the same hardships as his men. His battle speeches became legendary, instilling a fierce loyalty among his troops. With each victory, his legend grew, not only within the military ranks but also among the French citizenry.

The Italian campaign concluded with the Treaty of Campo Formio in 1797, which expanded French territories and marked France as the dominant power in Western Europe. Napoleon returned to France a national hero, his reputation bolstered by a well-managed propaganda campaign. His military genius, combined with his political acumen, had established him as a force to be reckoned with in the French political scene.

Yet, Napoleon's ambition was far from satisfied. In 1798, he set his eyes on a new objective, Egypt, hoping to disrupt British trade routes and establish a French presence in the Middle East. This campaign was not as successful as the Italian one and encountered numerous challenges. However, it further demonstrated Napoleon's audacity and ambition.

One of the most significant early milestones in Napoleon's career was his role in the coup of 18 Brumaire in 1799, which overthrew the French government, the Directory. The coup marked the end of the French Revolution and the beginning of Napoleon's political rule, as he became the First Consul of France.

Napoleon's early military career is marked by a relentless pursuit of excellence, innovative military strategy, and an uncanny ability to inspire loyalty. This period of his life laid the foundation for the formidable empire he would go on to build.

As we continue our journey through Napoleon's life in the upcoming chapters, we'll see how these early achievements played a significant role in his path towards ultimate power. So, let's turn the page and dive into the next chapter of this fascinating story.

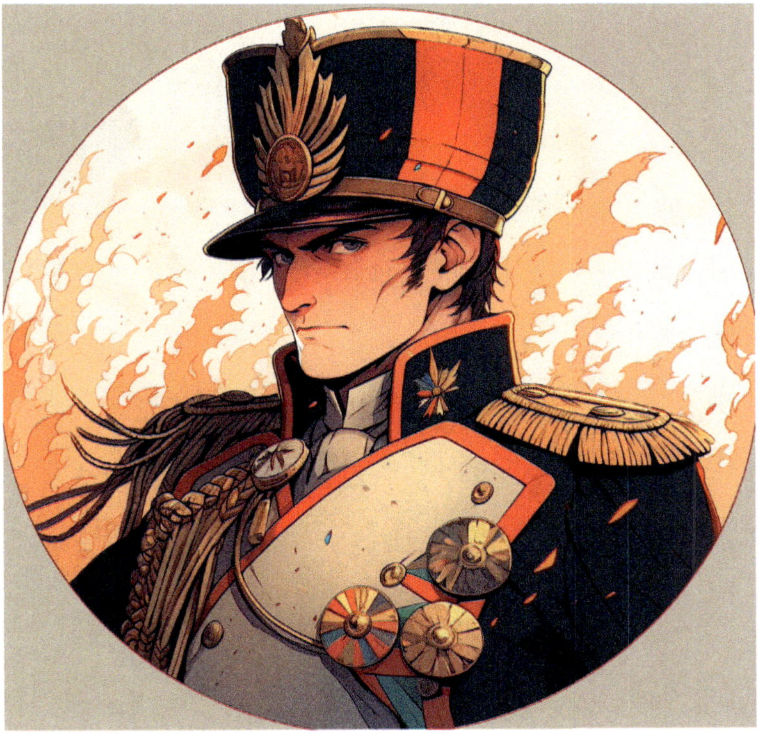

THE ITALIAN CAMPAIGN

Chapter 09

First Significant Military Campaign

Welcome back, dear reader! Today, we delve into one of the most pivotal chapters in Napoleon's remarkable life - the Italian Campaign. This chapter provides an in-depth look at Napoleon's first significant military campaign, marking the emergence of a military genius whose influence would reshape the continent.

In 1796, the French government, desperate for a victory, handed the command of the French Army of Italy to the 26-year-old Napoleon. The French forces were dispirited, under-equipped, and facing the superior forces of the Austrian and Piedmontese armies. It was under these circumstances that Napoleon set out on his Italian campaign, not as a daunting conqueror but as an ambitious young general with a point to prove.

Napoleon's strategy in Italy showcased his unique approach to warfare. He believed in rapid, aggressive strikes that divided and confused the enemy. His motto was "engage and then see," suggesting a flexibility and willingness to adapt that was uncommon in the rigid military thinking of the time.

The first significant victory came at the Battle of Montenotte in April 1796, where Napoleon's forces defeated the Austrians and their allies. He followed this success with a series of victories that forced Piedmont out of the war and pushed the Austrians back. The battles of Lodi, Castiglione, Bassano, and Arcole soon followed, each showcasing Napoleon's military genius and knack for motivating his troops.

A key factor in Napoleon's success was his personal leadership style. He often led from the front, inspiring his men with his courage and charisma. He also understood the value of morale and made sure to share in the hardships of his soldiers. His battle speeches became legendary and instilled a sense of purpose and loyalty among his troops.

The campaign reached its climax with the Battle of Rivoli in January 1797, where Napoleon's forces decisively defeated the Austrians, effectively ending their presence in Italy. After this victory, Napoleon negotiated the Treaty of Campo Formio with Austria, which marked the successful conclusion of the campaign and significantly expanded French territories.

The Italian Campaign was a remarkable achievement for Napoleon. It transformed him from a relatively unknown general into a national hero, and his innovative strategies revolutionized warfare. However, it was also a brutal campaign, characterized by widespread pillaging and harsh reprisals against partisan fighters.

The campaign's success laid the groundwork for Napoleon's future endeavors and established him as a master strategist. It was the first significant demonstration of his military genius and the precursor to the series of events that would lead him to unprecedented power. This ambitious young Corsican had shown the world he was not to be taken lightly.

So, dear reader, as we close the chapter on Napoleon's triumphant Italian Campaign, we stand at the precipice of a new era. Join me in the next chapter as we explore Napoleon's audacious attempt to conquer Egypt. Until then, happy reading!

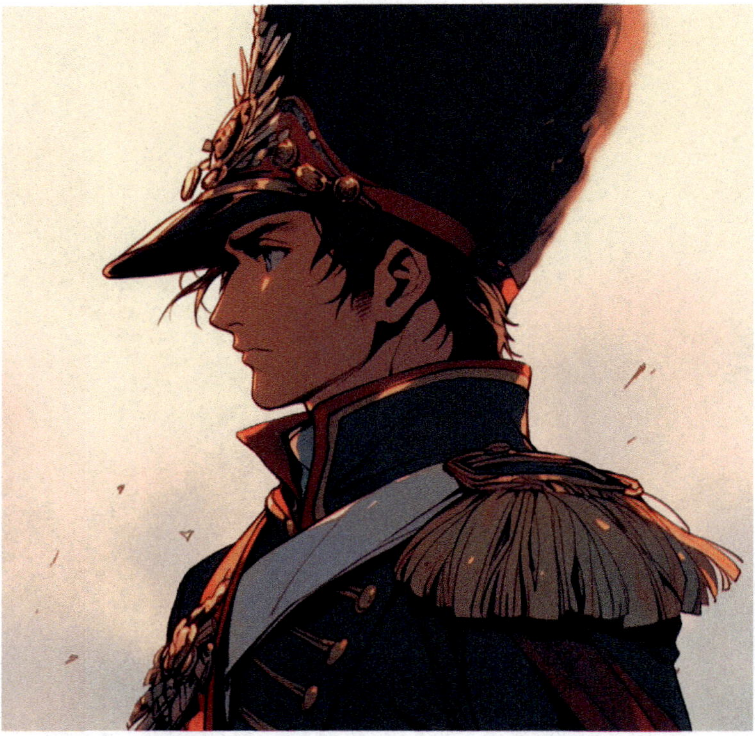

chapter 10

As a National Hero in France

Welcome back, dear reader! When we left off, Napoleon had just completed his successful Italian Campaign. The victories he achieved over the Austrian forces had resonated across Europe. Today, let's uncover how this ambitious Corsican general ascended from the chaos of war to become a national hero in his adopted homeland, France.

The late 18th century was a tumultuous time for France. The French Revolution had swept away the monarchy, replacing it with a republic that was constantly under threat, both internally and externally. France needed victories, not just to ensure its survival, but to boost the morale of its people and validate the ideals of the Revolution. It was within this context that Napoleon's triumph in Italy held such significance.

Napoleon's successes on the Italian front were a beacon of hope for France. Each battle won, each territory seized, brought not just strategic advantages, but also much-needed confidence. Through his swift and decisive military strategies, Napoleon was painting a picture of a new France, strong and defiant, on the European stage. The French people, in return, began to see him as a symbol of their resilience and the embodiment of their revolutionary spirit.

The timing of the Italian Campaign was also crucial to Napoleon's rise. Back home, the French government was struggling. The Directory, a five-man committee, was battling economic issues, civil unrest, and political infighting. France was in dire need of a unifying figure, a strong leader who could guide them through these troubled times. As news of Napoleon's victories trickled in, the general's stature grew. He was presented as the 'Savior of the Republic' and soon became the face of French success.

The young general was shrewd enough to grasp the importance of public image. While in Italy, he maintained a prolific correspondence with the French government and the press, narrating his victories, emphasizing his patriotic spirit, and showcasing his military genius. His dispatches were widely published and read aloud in public places, creating a larger-than-life image of the general, painting him as a hero of the people.

However, it wasn't just the victories that elevated Napoleon to the status of a national hero. It was the way he achieved them. His innovative strategies, personal bravery, and the care with which he treated his soldiers made him a beloved figure among his troops. This affection translated into popular support back home, creating a bond between the general and the common people of France.

Upon his return to France in 1797, Napoleon was greeted as a hero. The triumphant parade in Paris, filled with the jubilant faces of his compatriots, marked the moment when Napoleon, the general, truly became Napoleon, the national hero. His Italian Campaign had not just expanded France's territories and influence, but it had also given the French people a figure they could rally behind, a hero they could believe in.

As we close this chapter, it's clear that the Italian Campaign was more than just a military triumph. It was a turning point in Napoleon's life and in the history of France. It set the stage for Napoleon's political ascendency, which we'll delve into in the coming chapters. For now, dear reader, take a pause, let the echo of the Parisian cheers fade, and prepare for the next part of our journey through Napoleon's incredible life. Until then, happy reading!

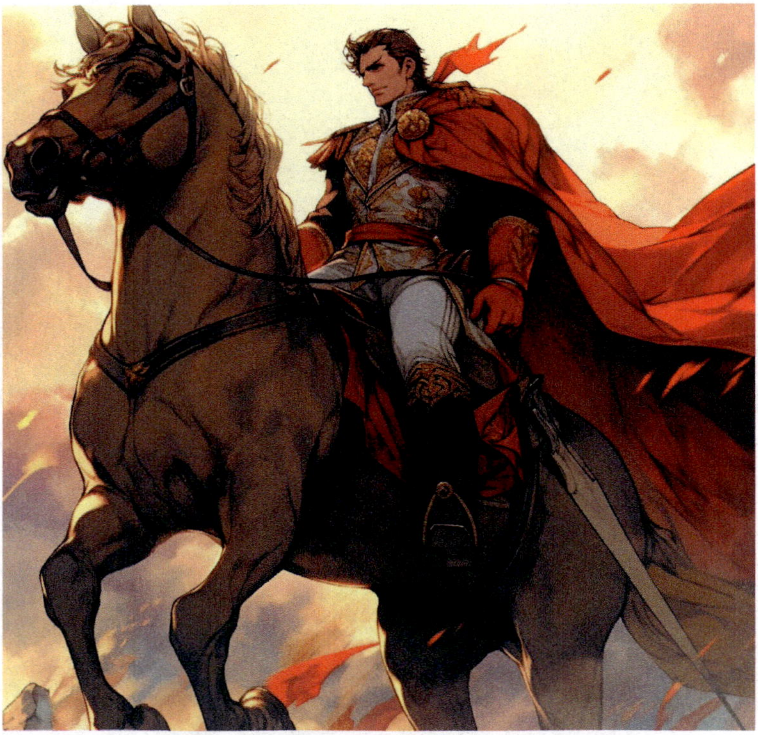

THE EGYPTIAN CAMPAIGN AND THE RISE TO POWER

chapter 11: Ambition to Conquer Egypt

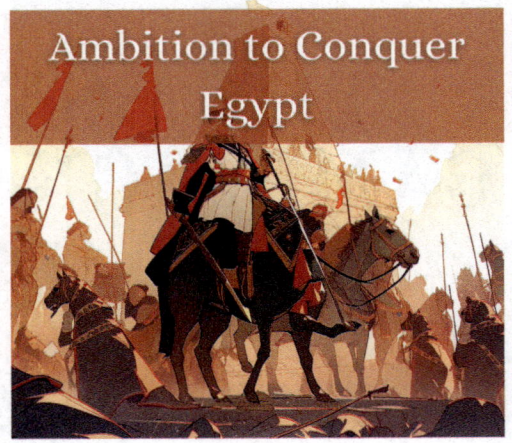

Hello again, dear reader! After exploring the rise of Napoleon to national hero status in the previous chapter, let's set sail on a new adventure to the mystical lands of the East, where the pyramids reach for the sky and the Nile waters hold ancient secrets. It was here, in Egypt, where Napoleon's ambitious vision saw an opportunity to create a legacy that would surpass all others. This chapter delves into the genesis and execution of that grand vision.

In the late 18th century, Europe's gaze was firmly fixed on the East. Spurred by tales of immense wealth, ancient wisdom, and strategic advantages, Eastern lands like Egypt held a tantalizing allure for the European powers. Napoleon was no exception. By 1798, with the victories of the Italian Campaign behind him, Napoleon was searching for his next conquest, a challenge that would not only elevate his stature but also benefit his beloved France. He found his answer in Egypt.

Napoleon's interest in Egypt was fueled by a mix of strategic considerations, scientific curiosity, and personal ambition. Strategically, controlling Egypt offered France a direct route to British India, the jewel in the crown of France's arch-enemy, the British Empire. Economically, Egypt, known for its fertile lands and key location, had the potential to become a prosperous French colony.

However, it wasn't just the strategic and economic benefits that drew Napoleon towards Egypt. The young general was deeply fascinated by the sciences and the arts. Egypt, with its rich history, archaeological treasures, and ancient knowledge, was like a treasure trove waiting to be explored. He dreamt of an Egypt where French scholars would uncover the secrets of the ancient world, heralding a new age of knowledge and understanding.

Furthermore, Napoleon was acutely aware of his public image. He understood that a successful campaign in Egypt would elevate him to legendary status, both in France and beyond. The image of Napoleon as the modern conqueror of Egypt, the land of the Pharaohs, would be a powerful symbol of his prowess and vision.

To turn his ambitious vision into reality, Napoleon assembled a large expeditionary force, not just composed of soldiers, but also scientists, engineers, and artists. This 'Armée d'Orient' was a testament to Napoleon's grand vision for Egypt - it was to be a conquest of not just land, but also of knowledge and culture.

However, ambition doesn't guarantee success, as Napoleon would soon discover. The Egyptian Campaign was fraught with difficulties, from resistance by local Mamluk rulers and British naval forces to the challenges posed by the harsh Egyptian climate. Despite these obstacles, Napoleon pressed on, driven by his unwavering ambition to conquer Egypt, a testament to his audacity and determination.

As we close this chapter, remember, dear reader, that ambition can often be a double-edged sword. On one hand, it pushes individuals to overcome daunting challenges, reach new heights, and often, change the world. On the other, unchecked ambition can lead to overreach, with dire consequences. The Egyptian Campaign, as we'll explore in the coming chapters, is a perfect example of this paradox of ambition.

So, let's keep our seatbelts fastened as we navigate through the complex tale of Napoleon's Egyptian Campaign in the subsequent chapters. Until then, immerse yourself in the visions of the pyramids and sphinxes, the roars of the French cannons, and the whispers of the Nile. See you in the next chapter, dear reader!

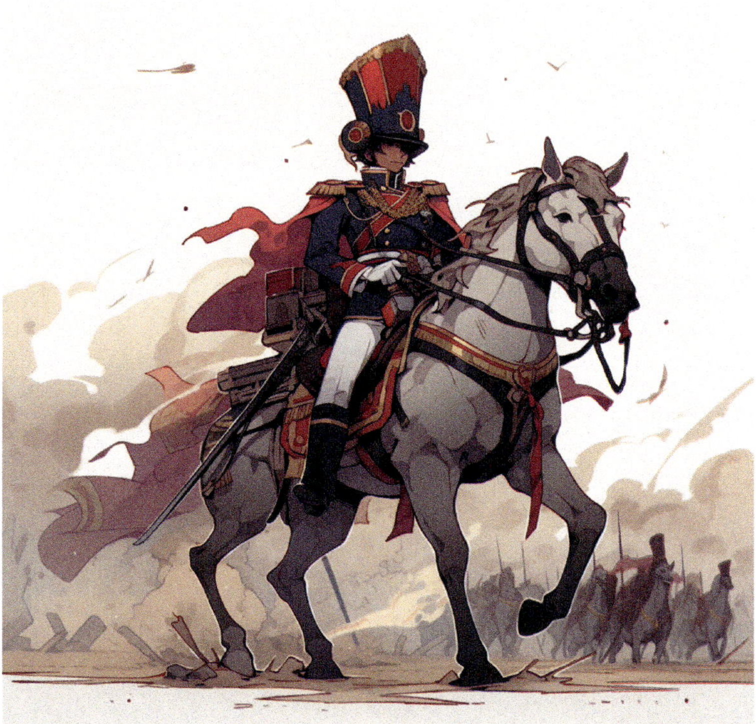

Chapter 12

The 'Liberator of the East'

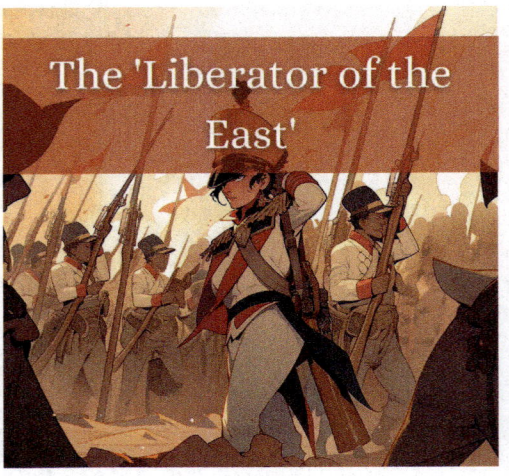

Hello there, dear reader! Welcome back as we continue to navigate the intriguing journey of Napoleon Bonaparte. Having charted his ambitions in our last rendezvous, let's now turn the pages towards an intriguing chapter of Napoleon's life - his self-proclamation as the 'Liberator of the East'.

In the shadows of the great Pyramids, along the ancient, silt-rich banks of the Nile, Napoleon would find an opportunity not only to expand France's empire but also to cast himself in a new, exalted role. From the sands of Egypt, Napoleon declared himself the 'Liberator of the East', a moniker that would elevate his standing and redefine his persona in the eyes of the Egyptian populace and beyond.

But why would Napoleon, a French general, claim such a title? Well, dear reader, as we've learned about our protagonist, he was not one to shy away from grand gestures or ambitious visions. The self-proclamation as the 'Liberator of the East' was a part of his broader strategy, as ingenious as it was audacious.

At the time, Egypt was under the rule of the Mamluks, a military caste originally composed of enslaved foreigners, who were often harsh in their governance. Napoleon, recognizing an opportunity, presented himself as a liberator who would free the Egyptians from Mamluk oppression. This was not just about winning the hearts and minds of the locals; it was also about creating an image of Napoleon as a leader and liberator, not just a conqueror.

To make this image believable, Napoleon adopted an interesting strategy. Upon entering Egypt, he showed respect for the Islamic religion and customs, even proclaiming that he himself was a follower of Islam. He ensured that his army respected places of worship and didn't interfere with the local customs and traditions.

Such respect for the culture and religion of the conquered territories was rare for European conquerors at the time. This strategy allowed Napoleon to build a narrative of liberation rather than invasion, an approach that earned him a certain degree of acceptance and respect among the Egyptian populace.

However, not everyone was taken in by this 'liberator' narrative. While some Egyptians saw him as a liberator, others saw him for what he was – a foreign invader. The British, too, were not fooled and recognized the strategic threat posed by Napoleon's presence in Egypt.

Self-proclamations are one thing; living up to them is another. Though Napoleon aimed to paint himself as the 'Liberator of the East', the realities of war, resistance from the locals, and international politics would prove this task to be more challenging than he had anticipated.

By the end of this chapter, dear reader, we see a more complex image of Napoleon - not just an ambitious conqueror, but also a savvy manipulator of public perception, a cultural diplomat of sorts. As we continue our journey into the following chapters, we'll see how this image and self-proclamation played out in the larger context of Napoleon's Egyptian Campaign and his rise to power. But that, my friends, is a tale for another day. Until then, let the mysteries of the East and the ambitions of Napoleon simmer in your minds. See you in the next chapter!

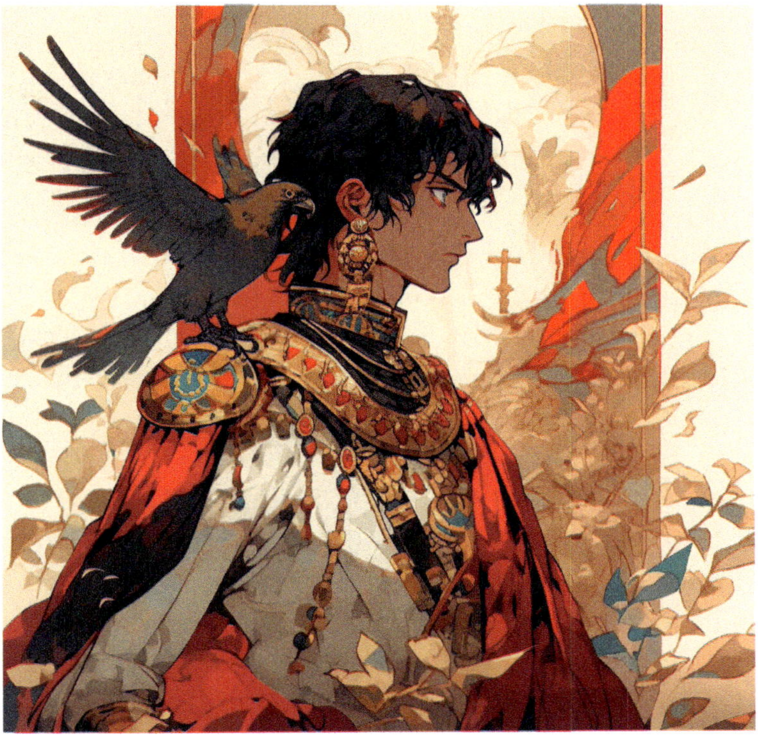

Chapter 13: The Coup that Catapulted Napoleon to Power

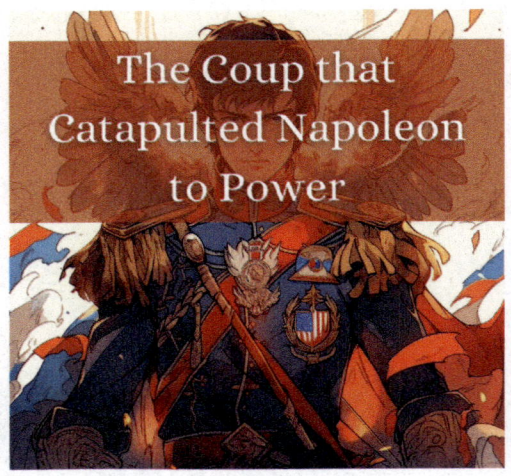

Hello again, dear reader! As we traverse the scintillating sands of time, we are reaching a crucial junction in our narrative - the coup that catapulted Napoleon to political power. But hold your horses; this isn't your run-of-the-mill palace coup; this is the stuff of legends, a masterstroke that forever shifted the political landscape of France.

To fully comprehend the significance of this coup, it's important to paint the picture of France at the close of the 18th century. After the initial fervor of the French Revolution had subsided, the country was politically unstable, financially bankrupt, and socially in disarray. A power vacuum had been created, ripe for a leader with charisma, determination, and vision to fill it. Enter Napoleon Bonaparte, fresh from his Egyptian adventures and hungry for power.

Having returned from Egypt after abandoning his campaign, Napoleon was well-aware that his military career would be under scrutiny. But as they say, fortune favors the bold, and Napoleon was nothing if not audacious. He turned this potential adversity into an opportunity, making his way to Paris, determined to seize power from the ruling Directory, a five-member committee that had proved to be ineffective and unpopular.

He aligned himself with his brother Lucien Bonaparte, who was the president of the Council of Five Hundred, and two Directors, Emmanuel Joseph Sieyès and Roger Ducos. Together, they planned a coup, dubbed the Coup of 18 Brumaire (named after the date in the French Republican Calendar), in November 1799.

The coup was a masterclass in manipulation, subterfuge, and power politics. The Council of Five Hundred was convening in Saint-Cloud, just outside Paris. There, Lucien Bonaparte, skillfully using his position as president of the Council, caused an uproar by claiming that the Council was under threat from extremists. At the height of this tumult, Napoleon was 'invited' to address the Council.

However, Napoleon's address went less smoothly than anticipated. He was met with hostility and even physical threats. In a dramatic turn of events, Lucien, thinking on his feet, rallied the troops outside the hall, claiming that his brother's life was in danger from the Council. The soldiers, loyal to Napoleon, stormed the Council chamber, effectively dispersing the representatives.

With the Council of Five Hundred disbanded, Napoleon, Lucien, Sieyès, and Ducos formed a new government, The Consulate. Napoleon, having shown himself to be the driving force behind the coup, was the obvious choice for the position of the First Consul, making him the de facto ruler of France.

As we close this chapter, dear reader, we find ourselves at a pivotal moment in our story. Napoleon Bonaparte, the military general from Corsica, has managed to seize political power in France through a daring coup. His ascension to power marked the end of the French Revolution and the beginning of a new era in French history. From this point forward, Napoleon wasn't just a military genius; he was a political juggernaut who would shape France and Europe for years to come.

But this is just the beginning of a new saga in Napoleon's life. Stay with me as we delve into the next chapter where we'll explore Napoleon's reign as the First Consul. Until then, let the audacity and cunning of Napoleon's coup d'etat keep your historical appetite whetted. See you in the next chapter!

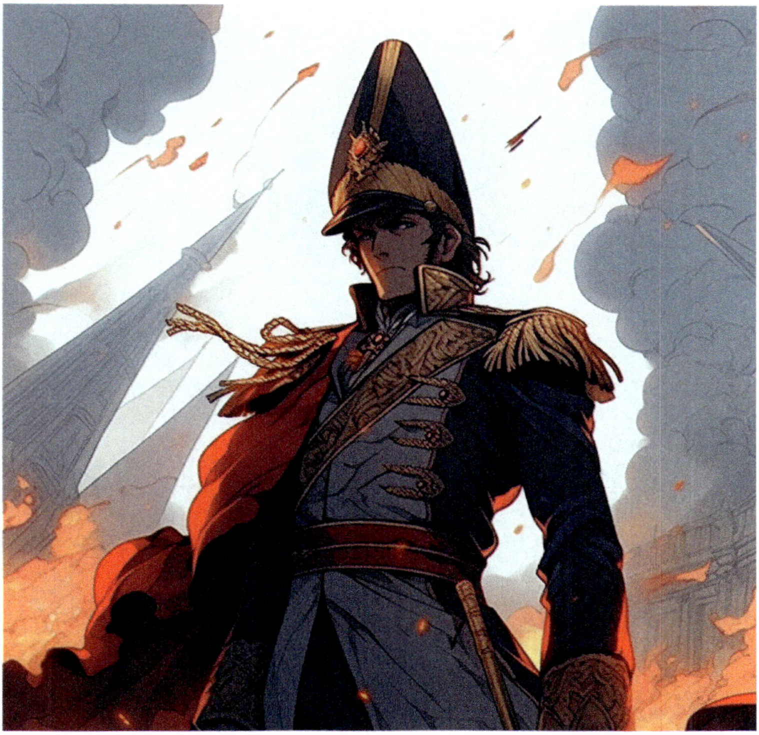

NAPOLEON AS FIRST CONSUL

Chapter 14: Napoleon's New Constitution

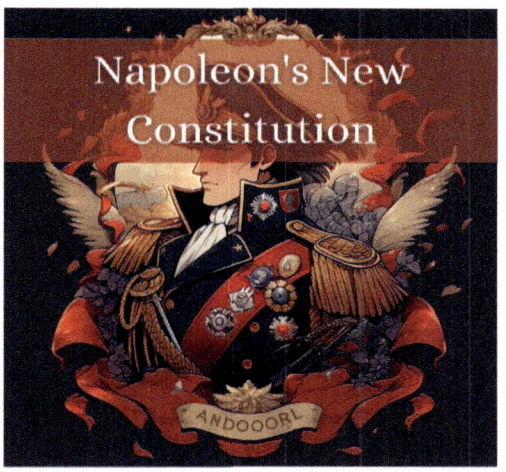

Welcome back, dear reader! As we journey through the vivid tapestry of Napoleon's life, we have now arrived at one of its most intriguing junctures - Napoleon's term as First Consul and his introduction of a new constitution. This period is more than just a historical footnote; it is, in essence, the birthing ground of Napoleon's era.

Just a quick recap to set the stage: After orchestrating the Coup of 18 Brumaire in 1799, Napoleon became the First Consul of France, effectively the ruler of the nation. Now, at the helm of affairs, Napoleon set out to accomplish what had eluded his predecessors - establishing a stable, effective government that won the confidence of the French people.

A crucial element of this was drafting a new constitution - the Constitution of the Year VIII (in the French Revolutionary Calendar), which was a testament to Napoleon's political acumen. Napoleon and his close advisers, including Emmanuel Joseph Sieyès, one of the co-conspirators of the coup, worked meticulously on this constitution, making it a vehicle for their vision of France.

While the constitution maintained the façade of a republic, it centralized power in the hands of three Consuls - First, Second, and Third. The First Consul, our protagonist Napoleon, wielded most of the executive power, a clever arrangement that satisfied the public's desire for a republic while giving Napoleon the power he craved.

On 15th December 1799, the Constitution of the Year VIII was approved by a public referendum, albeit amid allegations of voting irregularities. But hey, what's politics without a pinch of controversy, right?

Under the new constitution, the role of the First Consul was so empowered that Napoleon effectively became the political and military leader of France. While the Second and Third Consuls, Jean Jacques Régis de Cambacérès and Charles-François Lebrun respectively, had consultative roles, the actual decision-making power was firmly with Napoleon.

The constitution also created four assemblies - the Council of State, which drafted legislation; the Tribunate, which debated legislation without voting on it; the Legislative Assembly, which could not discuss legislation but voted on laws presented by the Council of State; and the Senate, which ensured that laws were constitutional. The ingenious part of this arrangement was that Napoleon appointed members to the Council of State and the Senate, maintaining control over legislation and its constitutional validity.

This new constitution marked a significant turning point in the history of France. It effectively brought an end to the political instability of the French Revolution and paved the way for Napoleon to consolidate power and enact far-reaching reforms in the years to come.

So, dear reader, as we close this chapter, we stand at the dawn of a new era in France under Napoleon. The introduction of a new constitution under his rule not only stabilized the nation but also laid the groundwork for his reign as Emperor, which we'll explore in the chapters to come.

Hang on tight, because the story of Napoleon, the crafty political leader, is just starting to unfold. Till we meet again in the next chapter, let the ingenuity and audacity of Napoleon's constitution fuel your imagination. Onward we march!

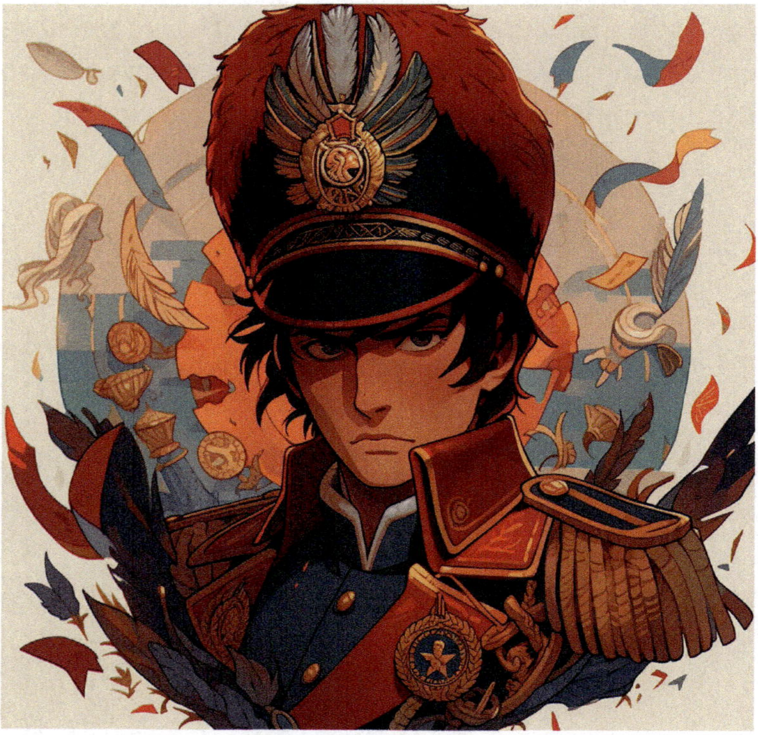

chapter 15

Law, and Society Under His Rule

Hello, dear reader! We've arrived at another important chapter in the remarkable story of Napoleon Bonaparte. Now that we've established how Napoleon shaped the political structure of France with a new constitution, let's delve into how he orchestrated pivotal reforms that dramatically altered French administration, law, and society.

Upon assuming the role of First Consul, Napoleon faced a France ravaged by a decade of revolutionary upheaval, with its administration in chaos, its law in disorder, and its societal structures unsteady. Far from being daunted, Napoleon saw an opportunity to build a robust, centralized administrative framework that would stabilize France and consolidate his own power.

A staunch believer in efficient bureaucracy, Napoleon initiated a host of administrative reforms. He divided France into 83 departments, each governed by a Prefect appointed by him. This resulted in a uniform administration across the country, ending the confusion caused by various local authorities. He also instituted a centralized tax collection system, making it more efficient and less prone to corruption.

In the sphere of law, Napoleon's most enduring contribution was the Civil Code, commonly known as the Napoleonic Code, implemented in 1804. This comprehensive legal framework aimed to sweep away the archaic laws and replaced them with a unified, modern system based on equality before the law and protection of civil liberties. It abolished feudalism and privileges based on birth, and affirmed the principles of property rights. The code was such a milestone that its basic tenets influence French law to this day and have been adopted in many other countries.

Education wasn't left untouched either. Believing that a well-educated citizenry was crucial to national progress, Napoleon overhauled the educational system. He established state-controlled schools known as 'lycées', which provided uniform education, primarily for boys, across the country. This reform not only improved education but also served as a tool for Napoleon to cultivate the future administrative and military leaders of France.

Another aspect Napoleon focused on was improving France's infrastructure. Roads, bridges, ports, and canals were built or renovated. The infrastructure projects not only stimulated the economy but also facilitated better military transport, a fact not lost on Napoleon, the strategic military leader.

Napoleon also reached out to the Catholic Church with the Concordat of 1801, ending a decade of bitter religious strife. While it reaffirmed religious freedom for all citizens, it also recognized Catholicism as the religion of the majority of the French, thereby winning him support from the Catholic populace.

In society, while Napoleon is often criticized for limiting women's rights in the Napoleonic Code and for his authoritarian rule, he brought a sense of order and stability that was a welcome change from the uncertainties of the Revolution. He is often remembered as a reformer who modernized France, setting it on the path to becoming the nation it is today.

So, there you have it, dear reader - a glimpse into how Napoleon, the First Consul, dramatically reshaped French administration, law, and society. As we close this chapter, we can reflect on the profound impact of these reforms. While some were controversial, their influence was undeniably far-reaching, resonating through the ages till today.

In our next chapter, we'll witness Napoleon's ultimate power move - his transition from First Consul to Emperor. Brace yourself, for the tale of Napoleon: The Conqueror, is far from over. Until then, let the enormity of Napoleon's reforms inspire thoughts and discussions. Bonne lecture!

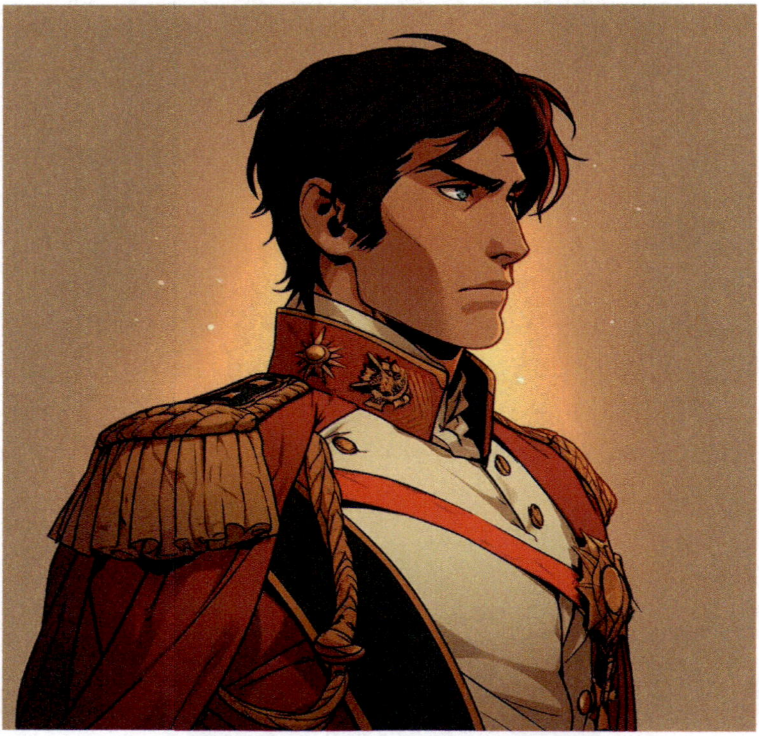

NAPOLEON AS EMPEROR

chapter 16

From First Consul to Emperor

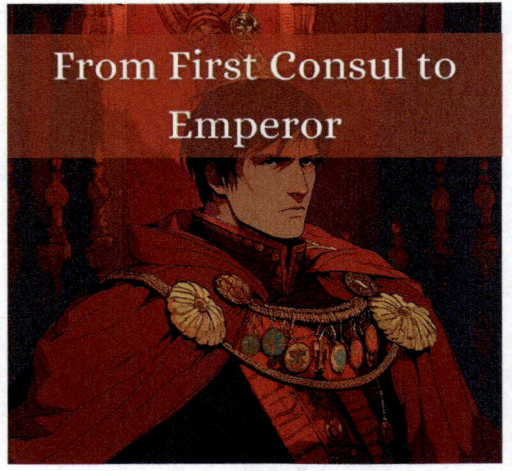

Hello again, dear reader! Today, we venture into one of the most significant phases of Napoleon's life, a period of unabated ambition and burgeoning power: the transition from First Consul to Emperor. So, sit back, relax, and join me on this grand journey as we traverse the path of Napoleon Bonaparte's ascension to the throne of France.

As we previously discussed, Napoleon's time as the First Consul was marked by a series of sweeping reforms that fundamentally altered the French political landscape, economic vitality, and societal fabric. Yet, even as he brought stability and prosperity to a country beleaguered by a decade of revolutionary turmoil, Napoleon harbored ambitions that transcended the bounds of the consulship.

So, how did Napoleon, the First Consul, become Napoleon, the Emperor? It was a journey marked not only by military prowess and administrative skill but also by political manoeuvring and careful orchestration of public sentiment.

In the wake of his successful rule as First Consul, Napoleon was already enjoying a level of power akin to that of a monarch. The French populace, weary of the chaos and uncertainty of the Revolutionary years, increasingly looked upon him as a figure of stability and order. Sensing the public mood, Napoleon began to consider a transition to hereditary rule, a move that would not only further consolidate his power but also secure the future of his regime.

The year 1804 marked the turning point. An alleged plot to assassinate Napoleon, often considered more of a pretense than a real threat, gave him the opportunity he needed. Using this as a justification, Napoleon proposed the establishment of a hereditary empire, with him at its helm. A subsequent plebiscite saw an overwhelming majority of the French vote in favor of the proposition. On 18th May 1804, the French Senate, largely a rubber-stamp body under Napoleon's control, proclaimed him Emperor of the French. The First Consul was no more; long live the Emperor!

But Napoleon wasn't content with just the title. He aimed to imbue his new status with a sense of divine legitimacy and historical continuity. Hence, on 2nd December 1804, in the grand Notre-Dame Cathedral, Napoleon was coronated as Emperor. In an iconic moment that symbolized his ultimate authority, Napoleon took the crown from Pope Pius VII and placed it on his own head. The message was clear: Napoleon owed his throne to no one but himself and the French people.

This audacious transition from First Consul to Emperor was more than just a change in title. It marked the end of one era and the beginning of another. It heralded the birth of the Napoleonic Empire, an era characterized by vast territorial expansion, persistent warfare, and enduring cultural impact. And at the heart of it all was Napoleon, the Emperor, a man of towering ambition and unmatched political acumen.

As we close this chapter, dear reader, consider the magnitude of Napoleon's ascent, from a minor Corsican noble to the Emperor of the French. His story, like the man himself, is larger than life. As we embark on the next phase of our journey, exploring his reign and the expansion of his empire, let's remember this moment of transition, for it is here that we truly witness the full measure of Napoleon: The Conqueror.

Till our next rendezvous, keep your curiosity alive and your passion for history kindled. Bonne lecture!

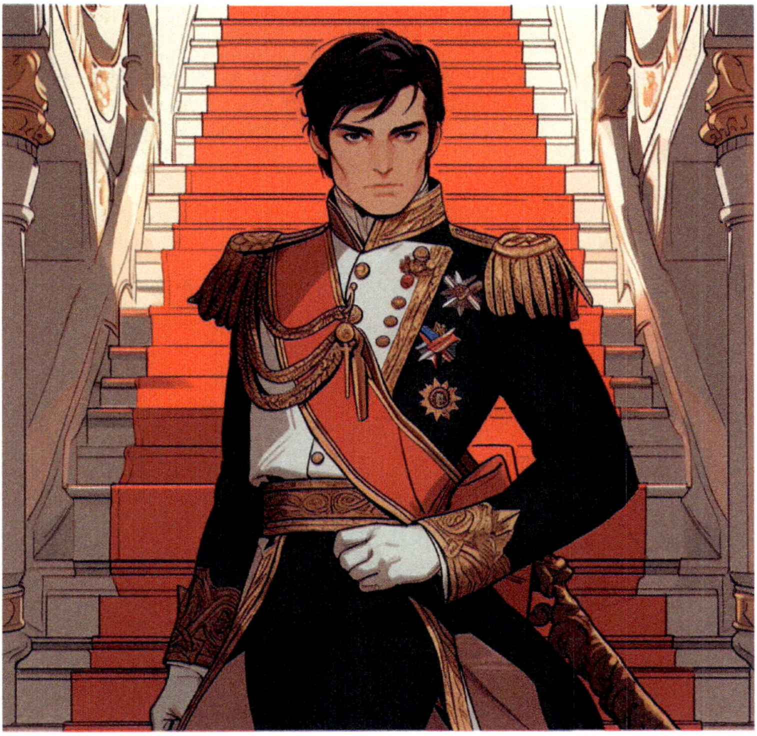

chapter 17

His Coronation and Reign

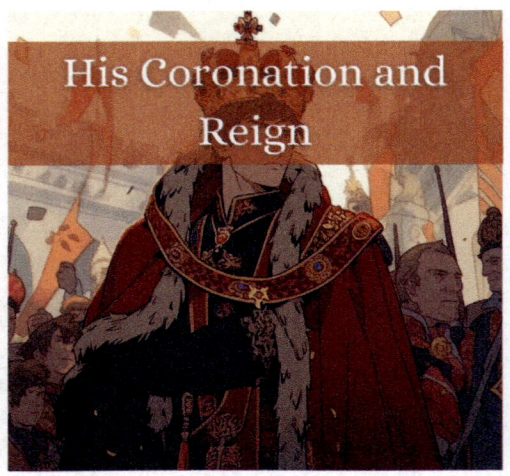

Hello again, dear reader! Welcome back to the grand narrative of Napoleon Bonaparte. Having just witnessed Napoleon's audacious transition from First Consul to Emperor, let us now turn our attention to one of the most lavish and symbolic events of his life: his coronation. We'll then proceed to his reign, a period of both monumental triumphs and escalating tensions.

As we learned in the previous chapter, Napoleon was declared Emperor on 18th May 1804. However, it was not until 2nd December that year that he truly assumed his imperial mantle, during a magnificent ceremony at the Notre-Dame Cathedral in Paris.

The coronation was an affair designed to impress and awe, from the intricate details of the imperial regalia to the sheer grandeur of the ceremony itself. In a break from tradition, Napoleon did not receive the crown from Pope Pius VII, who had been invited to preside over the ceremony. Instead, in a moment of supreme audacity, Napoleon took the crown and placed it upon his head himself. This act was symbolic, announcing to all that his power came directly from the people of France and not from any religious or traditional authority.

Now let us move forward from the pageantry of his coronation to the reality of his reign. Napoleon's reign was characterized by great military and administrative triumphs, but also by a growing centralization of power and the simmering tensions that came with it.

In terms of administration, Napoleon, the Emperor, was just as energetic and reformative as Napoleon, the First Consul. He continued to modernize the nation's administrative and legal systems, culminating in the creation of the famous Napoleonic Code, a civil law code that would have a long-lasting influence not only in France but across the world.

But there was more to Napoleon's reign than administrative reforms. As an emperor, Napoleon dreamed big. He sought to expand the boundaries of his empire and reshape the map of Europe. He embarked on a series of military campaigns, which, despite their mixed outcomes, indisputably marked him as one of history's greatest military strategists.

However, with great power came great challenges. The Napoleonic Empire was a vast territory encompassing diverse regions and peoples, and governing it was a Herculean task. Napoleon's policies, particularly the Continental System, caused friction with other major European powers, setting the stage for conflicts that would eventually lead to his downfall.

Despite these challenges, Napoleon's reign was a period of immense transformation for France and for Europe. It was a time of cultural blossoming, known as the Napoleonic Renaissance, when arts, sciences, and education flourished under his patronage. The institutions he built, the laws he enacted, and the societal reforms he implemented during his reign left an indelible mark on French society and continue to influence the world today.

As we delve deeper into the events of his reign in the subsequent chapters, remember, dear reader, that it is the complexities and contradictions of Napoleon's reign that make him such a fascinating figure. He was a man of paradoxes, capable of inspiring devotion and disdain, love and fear. But above all, he was Napoleon: The Conqueror, an individual who left an indelible mark on the pages of history.

So, keep your historian's hat on and your curiosity alive as we continue this grand journey into the life of one of history's most captivating figures. À la prochaine, dear reader!

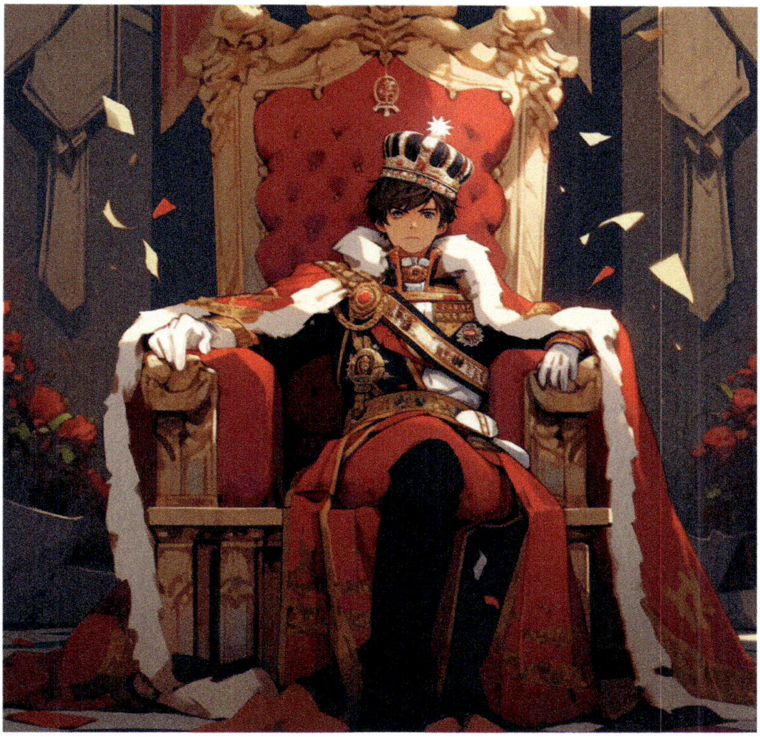

Chapter 18: French Empire Under His Leadership

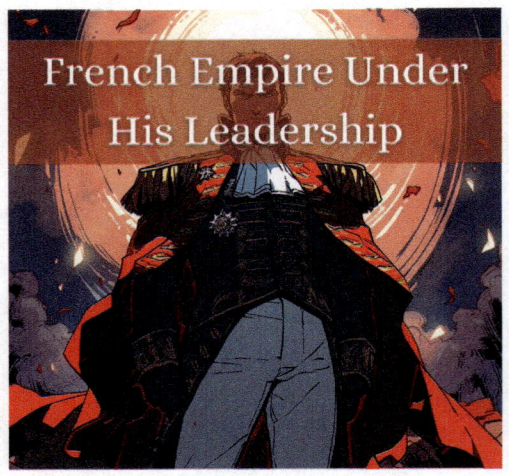

Hello again, dear reader! Isn't it fascinating to embark on a journey into the past and relive the moments that shaped our world today? In this chapter, we will accompany Napoleon on his grand voyage to expand the French Empire. So sit back, relax, and let's delve into this thrilling period of history together.

Napoleon Bonaparte, Emperor of the French, was not a man known for his modest ambitions. He had an insatiable desire for glory and power, which became evident in his imperial expansion policies. During his reign, the French Empire reached its greatest territorial extent, fundamentally altering the political landscape of Europe.

As you recall from previous chapters, Napoleon had already displayed his military genius in his early career, particularly during the Italian and Egyptian campaigns. His reign as Emperor allowed him to push his expansionist agenda even further.

The initial years of his rule saw swift territorial gains. He strategically placed members of his family and loyal allies as rulers of the conquered territories, ensuring their allegiance and securing French influence. This policy led to his siblings becoming kings and queens of newly formed or conquered regions such as Holland, Spain, Westphalia, and Naples.

Napoleon's ambition knew no bounds. His campaigns spread eastwards, stretching the Empire from Spain to the borders of Russia. The Battle of Austerlitz in 1805, often regarded as his greatest victory, resulted in the dissolution of the Holy Roman Empire and the establishment of the Confederation of the Rhine, a league of German states allied with France.

The Treaty of Tilsit in 1807, following the successful campaigns against Prussia and Russia, further expanded the French Empire and established Napoleon as the dominant figure in continental Europe. The map of Europe was being redrawn, with the French Empire and its dependent states as the primary power.

However, this expansion was not without its challenges. The vastness of the French Empire, its ethnic and cultural diversity, and the constant threat of rebellion and resistance from the conquered peoples presented a daunting task for Napoleon. The strain of maintaining this massive empire began to show, leading to overstretching of resources and exposing vulnerabilities.

Napoleon's Continental System, intended to cripple Britain's economy by closing European ports to British goods, had mixed results and added further strains. The trade blockade inadvertently harmed French and allied economies, leading to discontent among the French populace and its allies. More about this in the next chapter, so hold tight!

While Napoleon's expansionist policies brought him unprecedented power and glory, they also sowed the seeds of his downfall. The larger the Empire grew, the more enemies he made, leading to the formation of various coalitions against him.

In essence, the expansion of the French Empire under Napoleon's leadership was a tale of glory and doom, of great victories and crushing defeats. It changed the political and social fabric of Europe forever and set the stage for the tumultuous decades to follow.

As we venture forward into the dramatic final years of Napoleon's rule, remember this: history is not just about victories or defeats; it's about the aspirations of individuals and the immense impact they can have on the world. And so, our journey continues. À bientôt, dear reader!

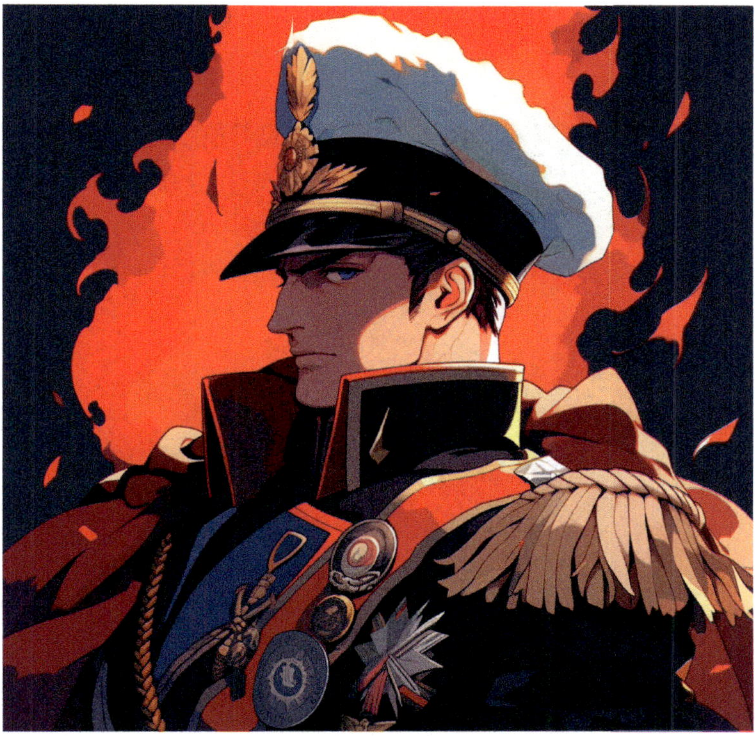

THE GRAND EMPIRE AND THE CONTINENTAL SYSTEM

Chapter 19

Grand Ambitions for Europe

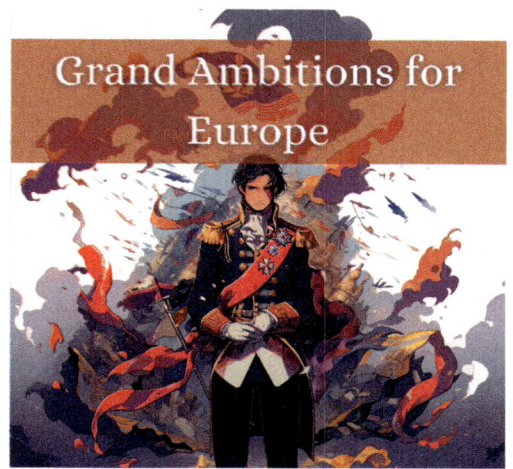

Hello again, dear reader! Aren't you amazed by the journey we have embarked on together? In this chapter, we'll delve deeper into Napoleon's ambitious vision for Europe, painting a vivid picture of his grand plans and the ways in which he attempted to reshape the entire continent. Let's set sail on this exciting voyage into the past.

By the time Napoleon ascended to the rank of Emperor, his ambitious nature had already led to the vast expansion of the French Empire, as we've seen in the previous chapter. However, his appetite for power was far from satiated. His dreams for Europe extended beyond territorial conquests; he aspired to restructure the entire European political, economic, and social order under his influence.

Napoleon's grand vision for Europe was primarily based on two cornerstones: the establishment of the Grand Empire and the implementation of the Continental System. His Grand Empire was a geopolitical entity that consisted of France, its dependent states, and allied states. Napoleon's intention was to mold Europe into a French-led confederation, guided by the ideals of the French Revolution: liberty, equality, and fraternity. At the same time, he sought to consolidate his rule by installing members of his family and close allies as rulers of various regions.

An essential aspect of Napoleon's grand ambition was the Continental System, which he believed would be the key to achieving complete domination over Europe, especially against his perpetual adversary, Britain. The system was essentially an economic weapon, a large-scale embargo against British trade. Napoleon aimed to cripple Britain's economy and force it into submission by cutting off its access to European markets. In essence, it was economic warfare, designed to complement his military campaigns.

However, implementing such an all-encompassing blockade was an enormous challenge. The Continental System was fraught with difficulties from the outset. It required the cooperation of all European states, many of which relied heavily on British goods or were reluctant to risk the wrath of the formidable British navy. Moreover, the blockade, in its stringent form, also adversely affected the economies of France and its allies, leading to widespread smuggling and discontent.

Nonetheless, the audacity of Napoleon's grand ambition is striking. Never before had a European leader sought to exercise such comprehensive control over the continent. His vision, albeit flawed and ultimately unsuccessful, was a testament to his strategic genius and his unyielding belief in his ability to reshape the world.

As we progress through our story, remember that history is not just a tale of successful ventures but also of grand failures. Napoleon's ambitious plans for Europe were as much a part of his legacy as his victories on the battlefield. His story reminds us of the immense potential, and peril, of human ambition.

So, dear reader, let's continue to walk the tightrope of history, exploring the triumphs and tragedies that marked Napoleon's rule. On to the next chapter, where we shall explore the Continental System in more detail. See you there!

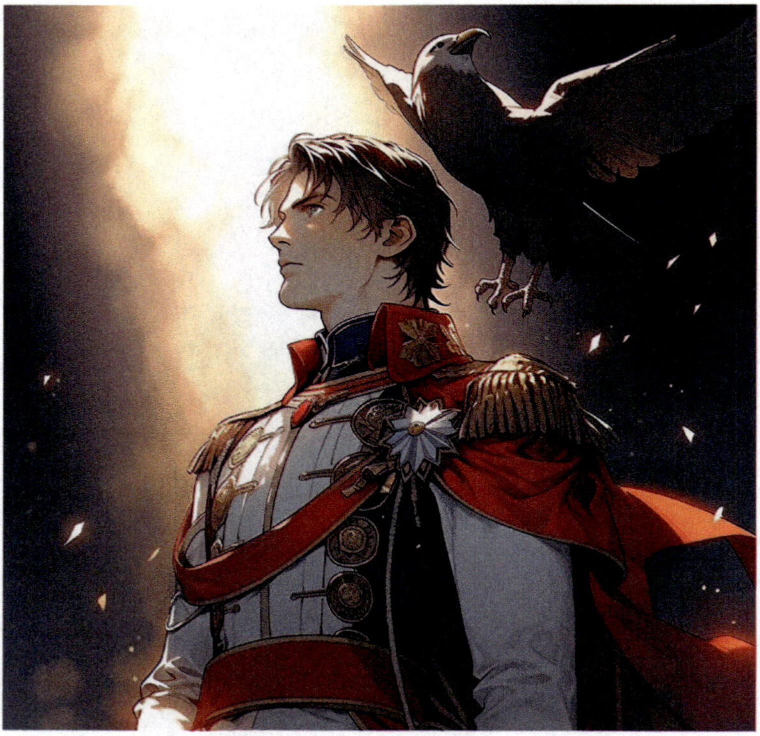

Chapter 20: The Continental System

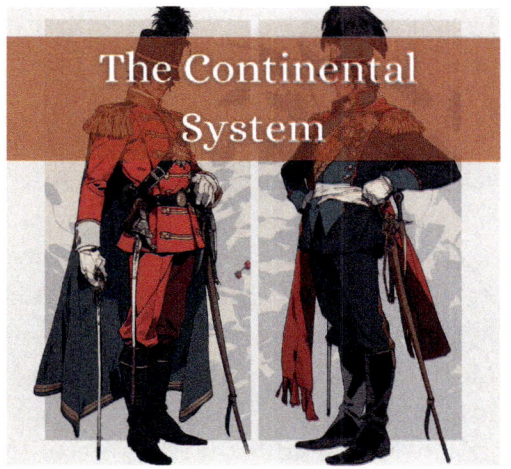

Hello again, dear reader! I hope you're ready for another deep dive into the history of Napoleon's reign. Remember our last rendezvous where we discussed Napoleon's grand ambitions for Europe? This time, we'll be focusing on the implementation of the infamous Continental System, an economic policy that shaped the destinies of nations and played a pivotal role in the rise and fall of the Napoleon Empire. So, let's embark on this new adventure together!

As we've previously noted, Napoleon sought to weaken Britain, his perpetual nemesis, through the Continental System, which was essentially an economic blockade. In 1806, Napoleon issued the Berlin Decree, marking the formal inception of the Continental System. The decree forbade the importation of British goods into European nations allied with or dependent upon France, and installed customs officials at various ports to enforce this ban.

In theory, the Continental System seemed like an ingenious strategy. After all, by denying Britain access to European markets, Napoleon hoped to cripple its economy, thus indirectly conquering a foe he could not vanquish on the battlefield. However, implementing such a grand scheme was far more complicated than it appeared.

At the heart of the challenge was the fact that the Continental System required unwavering cooperation from all of Europe. Many nations bristled at the restrictive trade policy, which impacted their own economies adversely. While countries under Napoleon's direct control had little choice but to comply, others—most notably Russia—proved more resistant. The Tzar of Russia, an important player in Napoleon's European stage, began to defy the Continental System in 1810, allowing British goods into Russia and setting the stage for dramatic conflict, as we'll see in later chapters.

Moreover, smuggling became rampant across Europe. From coastal towns in Spain to bustling ports in the Baltic, covert trade networks blossomed. Unsurprisingly, it was an uphill battle for French officials to monitor and control every single port and border.

The impact on the French economy and its allies was also significant. The economies of these nations relied on trade, and the sudden restriction caused economic stagnation and widespread discontent among the populace and merchants, who missed the variety and quality of British goods.

While the Continental System did have some effect on the British economy, it was not the crippling blow Napoleon had hoped for. Britain, in response, tightened its naval blockade of France, disrupting French trade even further and leading to a series of events that would eventually escalate into the Peninsular War.

As we take a step back and assess the grand tapestry of Napoleon's reign, we see the Continental System as an emblem of his ambition, audacity, and even his hubris. It represented his attempt to subjugate not just the nations of Europe, but the currents of commerce and the tides of the sea themselves.

But remember, dear reader, that in history, as in life, nothing is ever simply black and white. In the next chapter, we'll delve into the consequences of the Continental System, and the complex web of cause and effect it wove across Europe. Until then, keep your curiosity alive and your spirit for learning aflame!

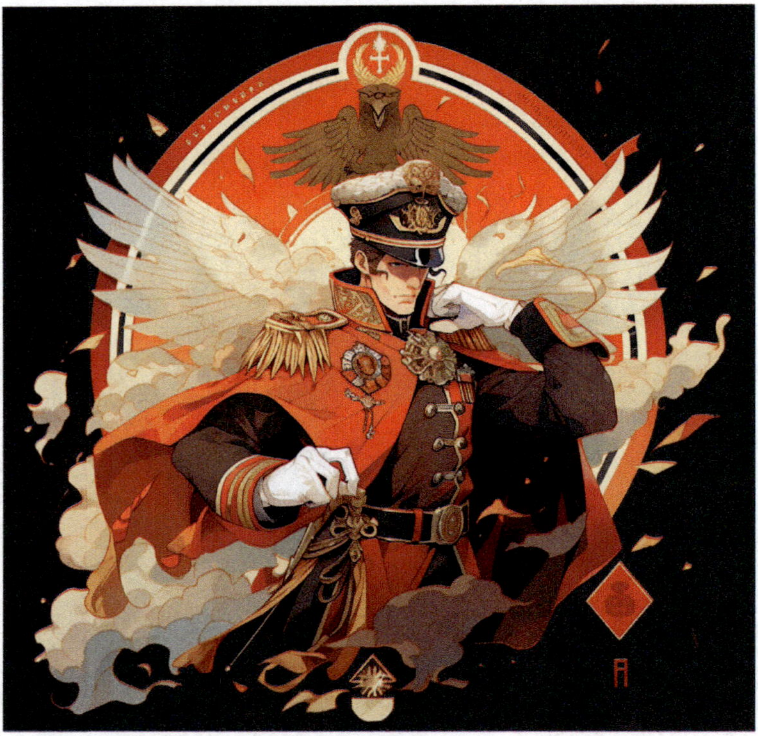

Chapter 21

The Effects of His Policies on Europe

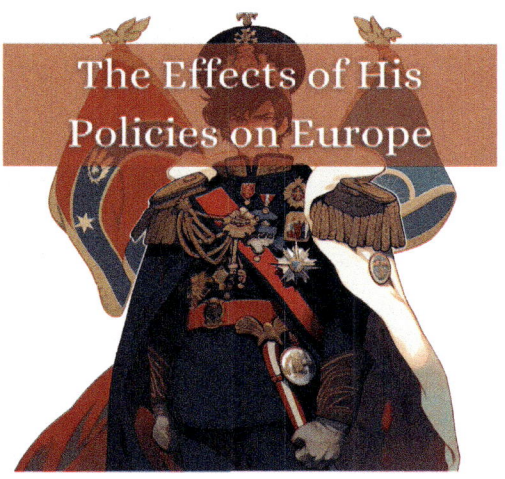

Greetings once more, dear reader! Our journey through the life of Napoleon Bonaparte continues, and today we find ourselves exploring the rippling effects of his policies across the great expanse of Europe. I invite you to join me on this exciting venture as we unveil the intricate web of cause and effect spun by the policies of the French Emperor, particularly the Continental System.

Napoleon's reign marked a period of seismic shifts in the European landscape, both politically and economically. The Continental System was a cornerstone of his grand strategy, an ambitious attempt to curtail Britain's economic power. However, the policy's effects on the continent were widespread and multifaceted, and, as often happens with such grand designs, not always as intended.

To begin with, the economic repercussions were profound and far-reaching. Many European countries relied heavily on trade with Britain. The blockade disrupted this trade, leading to stagnation, a rise in the prices of goods, and even famine in certain regions. The textile industries in Belgium and Germany, for instance, were heavily affected by the scarcity of raw materials, predominantly cotton, which was primarily imported from British colonies.

Likewise, countries like Russia, who had significant trade ties with Britain, were unwilling to harm their own economies to comply with Napoleon's dictates. This ultimately led to a severe rift between Napoleon and Tsar Alexander I of Russia, setting the stage for the catastrophic French invasion of Russia in 1812.

Moreover, the Continental System fostered a surge in smuggling and illicit trade across Europe, creating a parallel economy and deepening the chasms of inequality. From the forests of Eastern Europe to the craggy coastlines of Spain, illicit trade networks thrived, often with the tacit or explicit support of local populations who bore the brunt of the economic hardships.

At a broader level, Napoleon's policies, including the Continental System, altered the very structure of European politics and society. His Napoleonic Code brought reforms that forever transformed legal systems across the continent. His establishment of 'sister republics' in countries like Italy, Holland, and Spain marked an assertion of French hegemony that stoked the flames of nationalism in these regions.

It's crucial to note that the impacts of Napoleon's policies weren't solely negative. His legal and administrative reforms brought a degree of uniformity and modernity to the bureaucracies of various European states. Moreover, his promotion of secularism and equality before the law were transformative ideas that outlived his reign and became foundational principles of many European nations.

So, what do we make of all this, dear reader? Like any potent force in history, Napoleon left an indelible mark on the landscape of Europe, a mark etched with the implements of war, trade, law, and administration. His policies were an intriguing mix of ambition, pragmatism, and sheer audacity that continue to intrigue historians and history enthusiasts alike.

In the chapters that follow, we'll examine the final years of Napoleon's rule, the unraveling of his empire, and the profound legacy he left behind. So, hang on to your hats, for our exploration of the Napoleonic age is far from over!

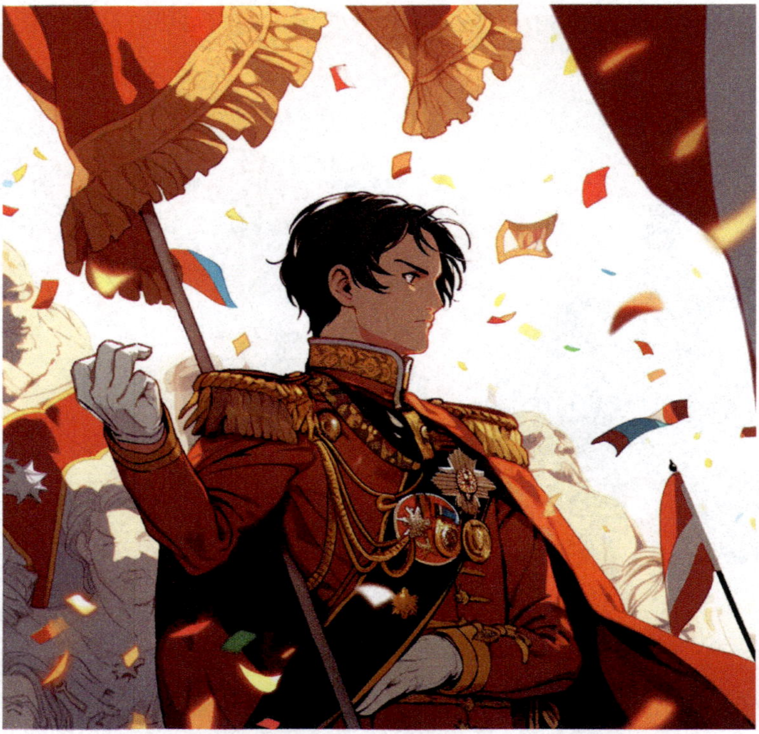

DOWNFALL: THE INVASION OF RUSSIA

Chapter 22

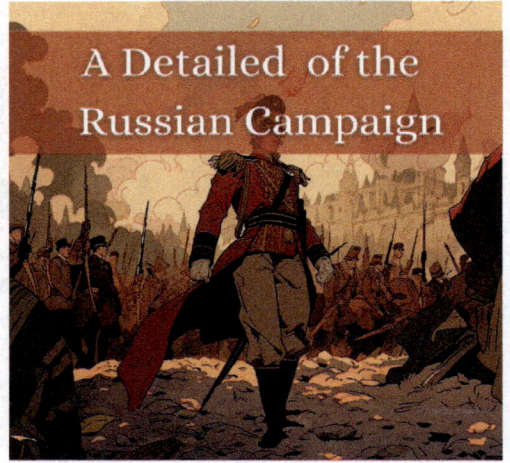

A Detailed of the Russian Campaign

Hello once again, my fellow historical voyagers! As we've traced Napoleon's meteoric rise, it's time now to pivot and delve into the campaign that marked the beginning of the end for the French Emperor: the disastrous invasion of Russia in 1812. Fasten your seatbelts, and prepare for a whirlwind tour through this pivotal moment in European history.

It was the year 1812, and the stage was set for one of the most significant military campaigns in history. Napoleon, the master tactician and conqueror of Europe, was up against Tsar Alexander I, the ruler of the vast Russian Empire. At the heart of the conflict lay Napoleon's Continental System and the Russian refusal to comply with it, but beneath the surface, this was also a struggle between two powerful leaders, each determined to assert his dominance.

The Grande Armée, Napoleon's pride and joy, entered Russia in June 1812 with approximately 680,000 soldiers. It was the largest army Europe had ever seen. Full of confidence and determination, they marched towards Moscow, expecting a swift victory. But as we well know, history had other plans.

The Russian strategy, devised by General Mikhail Kutuzov, was one of "scorched earth". As Napoleon's forces advanced, the Russians retreated, burning crops, villages, and towns in their wake, denying the French any chance of living off the land. The vast Russian landscape, coupled with this strategy, stretched Napoleon's supply lines to breaking point.

The Battle of Borodino in September 1812 was the single deadliest day of the campaign. Despite severe losses on both sides, the French army was ultimately victorious. Napoleon finally reached Moscow, only to find it ablaze. The Russians had torched their own capital to deprive the French of supplies and shelter. The dream of a quick victory turned into a nightmarish reality for Napoleon and his men.

As winter descended, the situation for the Grande Armée grew dire. Starvation, hypothermia, disease, and Russian raids decimated the French forces. Napoleon, realising the extent of the catastrophe, decided to retreat. This retreat, conducted in the harsh Russian winter, has been etched into history as a symbol of defeat and devastation. Out of the original 680,000 men, only about 27,000 combat troops returned.

The Invasion of Russia exposed flaws in Napoleon's strategic thinking. His overreliance on the 'battle of annihilation' — the belief that a decisive, crushing victory could compel his adversary to capitulate — did not work against the Russians. His inability to adapt his tactics to the harsh Russian conditions and the tenacity of the Russian people marked a turning point in his fortunes.

The impact of this campaign extended far beyond Russia and France. It signaled to the rest of Europe that Napoleon was not invincible. His aura of invincibility shattered, coalitions that had previously been defeated by Napoleon saw a chance for revenge. The stage was set for the War of the Sixth Coalition, which would ultimately drive Napoleon to abdication.

So, dear readers, we leave this chapter with a stark reminder of the often cruel, unpredictable nature of war. The same Napoleon who had stood victorious in so many European capitals, found his match in the vast, icy expanses of Russia. The 'Napoleonic Sun' had started to set, and the landscape of Europe would never be the same. In our following chapters, we'll explore the final twists and turns of this incredible story. Stay tuned!

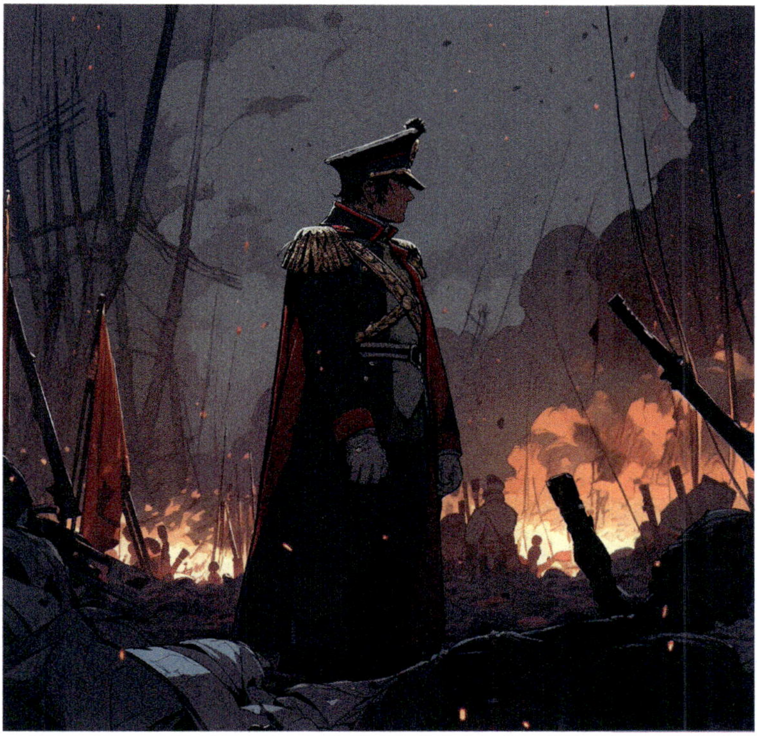

Chapter 23: Napoleon's Strategic Errors

Hello, dear readers! As we navigate through the intricate maze of Napoleon's life and legacy, we've reached a pivotal moment where our ambitious protagonist takes a misstep, resulting in far-reaching consequences. Today, let's delve into Napoleon's strategic errors and misjudgments during his ill-fated Russian Campaign.

Even the greatest of minds can fall prey to errors, and Napoleon, despite his military genius, was no exception. As we've seen in the previous chapter, the invasion of Russia in 1812 was a catastrophic defeat for Napoleon. A few key missteps turned what he hoped would be a crowning glory into a disastrous retreat.

Underestimating Russia's Resistance

First and foremost, Napoleon severely underestimated the Russian resolve to resist his invasion. He expected Tsar Alexander I to sue for peace after a decisive battle or two. This assumption was based on his past experiences in Europe, where he had achieved quick victories against other monarchies. However, he failed to account for Russia's unique geopolitical circumstances and the resilience of the Russian people, who proved willing to endure great hardships to resist his forces.

Failure to Account for the Russian Winter

Napoleon's failure to plan for the harsh Russian winter was a critical mistake. He launched the invasion in June, expecting a swift victory before winter. However, the Russian 'scorched earth' policy and their strategic withdrawals extended the campaign far longer than he anticipated. By the time Napoleon reached Moscow in September, winter was around the corner. Napoleon was ill-prepared for the brutal Russian winter, which led to the loss of tens of thousands of men due to cold, starvation, and disease.

Overextended Supply Lines

Napoleon's Grand Armée was the largest army ever assembled in European history, making logistics a nightmare. The 'scorched earth' policy implemented by the Russians meant that the French could not live off the land, exacerbating the problem of overextended supply lines. This led to shortages in food and other essential supplies, further weakening Napoleon's forces.

Relying on a Single Decisive Battle

Napoleon's battle plan relied on a strategy of drawing the Russian forces into a single decisive battle, where he could annihilate them and force the Tsar to negotiate. This had worked in his previous campaigns in Europe, but in Russia, this plan fell apart. The Russians avoided such a battle, engaging in smaller, costly engagements such as the Battle of Borodino, which, despite being a technical victory for Napoleon, failed to yield the decisive result he hoped for.

Underestimating the Psychological Impact

Lastly, Napoleon underestimated the psychological impact of the Russian campaign on his troops and his reputation. The disastrous retreat from Moscow shattered the aura of invincibility that had surrounded Napoleon, demoralizing his army and emboldening his European adversaries.

In conclusion, even a leader of Napoleon's caliber was not immune to errors of judgment. His strategic mistakes in the Russian Campaign marked a turning point in his reign, revealing that the emperor was fallible after all. These missteps offer a valuable lesson that even the most powerful and intelligent leaders can falter when they overreach, underestimate their enemies, and fail to adapt to changing circumstances.

Stay tuned, dear readers, as we move closer to the finale of Napoleon's epic saga. We'll explore his subsequent exile, return, and final defeat in the coming chapters.

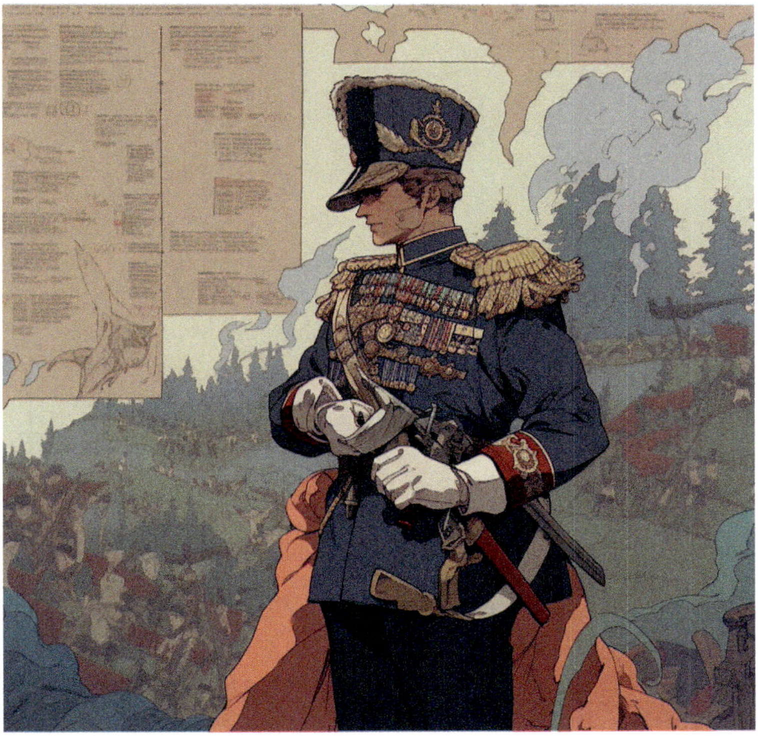

EXILE, RETURN, AND FINAL DEFEAT

Chapter 24: Return during the Hundred Days

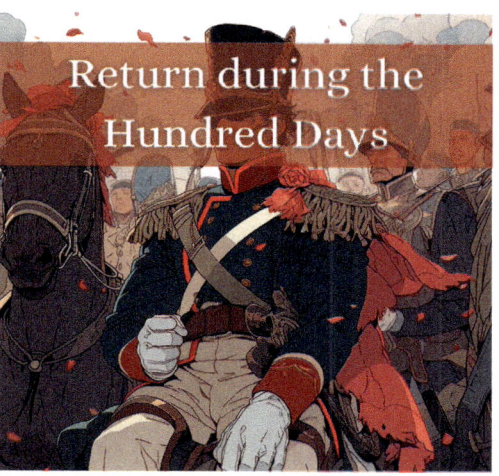

Hello again, dear reader! As we embark on this penultimate chapter of Napoleon's life story, we find ourselves on the shores of a small island off the coast of Italy: Elba. Following his catastrophic campaign in Russia, Napoleon was forced to abdicate his throne and was exiled to this tiny island. But as we know, our protagonist wouldn't stay out of the limelight for long. He would stage a dramatic comeback before meeting his final defeat at Waterloo.

Elba: The First Exile

Napoleon's abdication in 1814 marked the end of his reign as the Emperor of France. He was granted sovereignty over the island of Elba, which became his little empire. Here, he spent his days in an absurd parody of his former imperial life, with an army of 1,000 men and a small navy. It was a peaceful existence, but one that didn't satisfy Napoleon's restless spirit and ambition. He missed his former life, the thrill of power, and most importantly, the rush of battle.

The Hundred Days: The Comeback

The French political landscape soon shifted in Napoleon's favor. Louis XVIII, the new Bourbon king, was unpopular with the French people and the army, creating an opening for Napoleon. On February 26, 1815, after less than a year in exile, Napoleon escaped from Elba and returned to France. His return, known as the 'Hundred Days,' was marked by a surge of public support. The army welcomed him back with open arms, and he was able to march into Paris unopposed, retaking the throne with ease.

Waterloo: The Final Defeat

However, this restored glory was short-lived. Europe declared war on Napoleon, culminating in the Battle of Waterloo in June 1815. The battle was fiercely fought, with Napoleon demonstrating his tactical genius once again. But this time, he faced two formidable adversaries: the British, led by the Duke of Wellington, and the Prussians, under Gebhard von Blücher.

Napoleon's decision to delay the start of the battle, coupled with the arrival of the Prussian reinforcements, proved disastrous. The French were finally defeated, and Napoleon's last chance to regain his empire was lost.

Aftermath of Waterloo

After Waterloo, Napoleon was once again forced to abdicate. He intended to flee to America, but the British intercepted him. Instead of the relative comfort of Elba, this time, his exile would be on Saint Helena, a remote island in the South Atlantic, far from the power centers of Europe.

So, dear reader, we leave Napoleon at the end of this chapter in a humbler setting than he was accustomed to. But his story is far from over. He may have been defeated, but his influence lived on, shaping the course of history long after his death. In the next chapter, we'll explore his final years on Saint Helena and his enduring legacy.

Stay tuned for the concluding chapter of this incredible journey through the life of Napoleon Bonaparte, a man whose name remains synonymous with power, ambition, genius, and, as we've seen in this chapter, defeat.

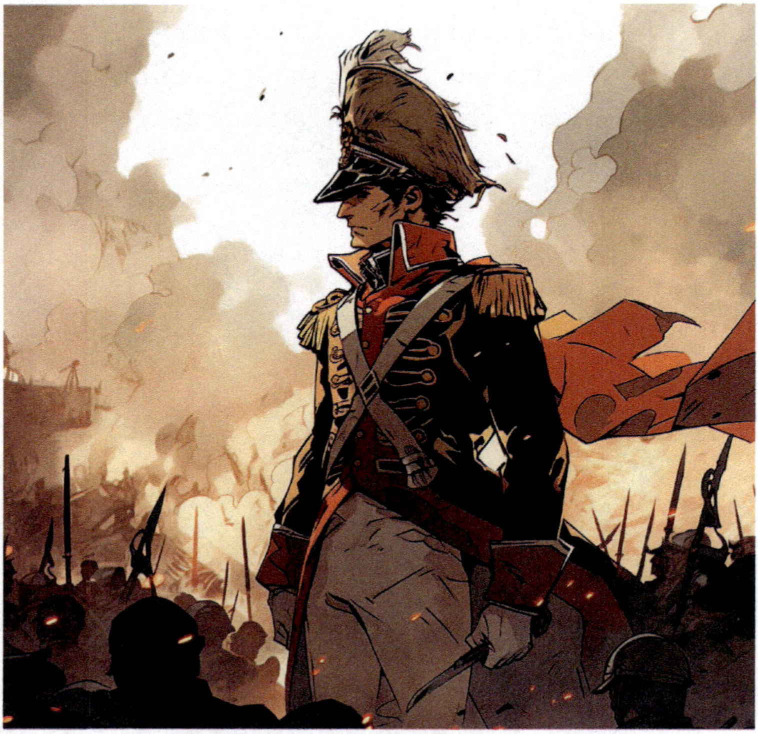

Chapter 25

Final Exile to Saint Helena

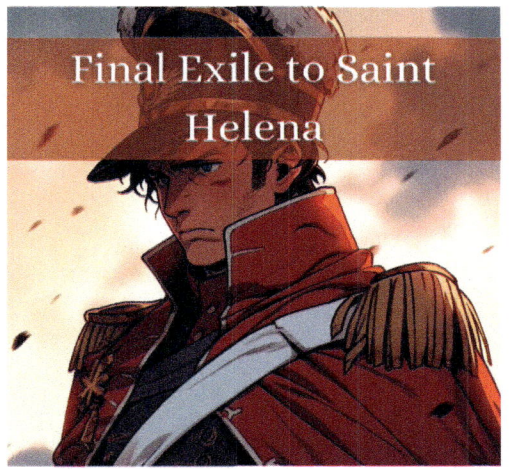

Hello again, dear reader. As we continue on our journey through the extraordinary life of Napoleon Bonaparte, we've arrived at his final years. After his dramatic return to power and subsequent defeat at Waterloo, Napoleon was exiled for the last time, not to the relative comfort of Elba, but to the remote island of Saint Helena. It was here that he would spend his final years, far from the land and people he had once ruled.

Saint Helena: The Final Exile

In the aftermath of the Battle of Waterloo, the British decided that Napoleon should be confined where he could no longer disrupt European peace. This led them to choose Saint Helena, a tiny, windswept island in the South Atlantic, more than a thousand miles from any major landmass. It was an effective, if harsh, solution.

In October 1815, Napoleon was transported to this remote outpost on the ship HMS Bellerophon. His new residence was Longwood House, a damp and windswept dwelling that was a far cry from the grandeur of the palaces he had known in his heyday.

Life on Saint Helena

Life on Saint Helena was a radical departure from anything Napoleon had experienced before. Gone were the grand receptions and military parades. Instead, he passed his days in relative solitude, occupying his time with gardening, reading, and writing his memoirs.

These memoirs would later become a valuable resource for historians, providing intimate insights into his rise to power, his reign, and his ultimate downfall. Despite his isolation, Napoleon never lost his sharp mind and continued to keep abreast of European affairs, using a limited supply of books and newspapers.

Declining Health and Death

Napoleon's health gradually declined during his years on Saint Helena. He complained of various ailments, including stomach pains, which many historians now believe may have been symptoms of stomach cancer. Despite his failing health, he remained intellectually active until the end. On May 5, 1821, Napoleon Bonaparte died at Longwood House, officially of stomach cancer, though some disputed this cause and suspected poisoning.

Legacy

Although the last chapter of Napoleon's life was marked by defeat and isolation, it did little to diminish his reputation. If anything, his exile only served to enhance the legend of Napoleon. His death transformed him from a deposed emperor into a romantic figure, a symbol of military genius and national pride.

As we prepare to conclude our journey through the life of Napoleon in the next chapter, we are reminded that even in defeat and exile, he remained a formidable figure, a man whose legacy continued to shape the world long after his death.

Stay tuned, dear reader, for our final chapter. We'll delve into the long-term effects of Napoleon's rule in France and Europe, and how he shaped the course of world history. We will explore how Napoleon, in victory and defeat, in power and in exile, left an indelible mark on the world.

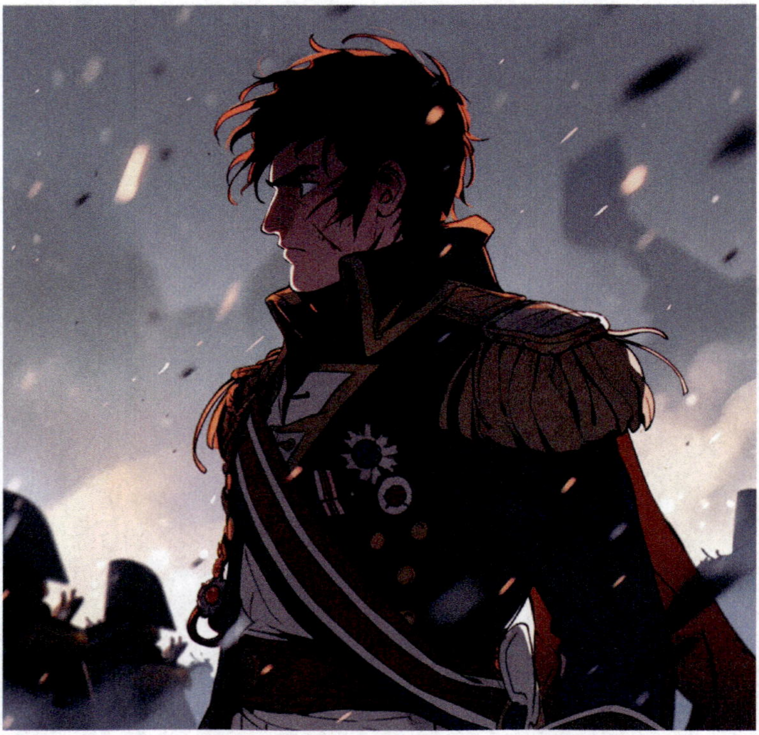

LEGACY AND CONCLUSION

Chapter 26: The Long-Term Effects of Napoleon

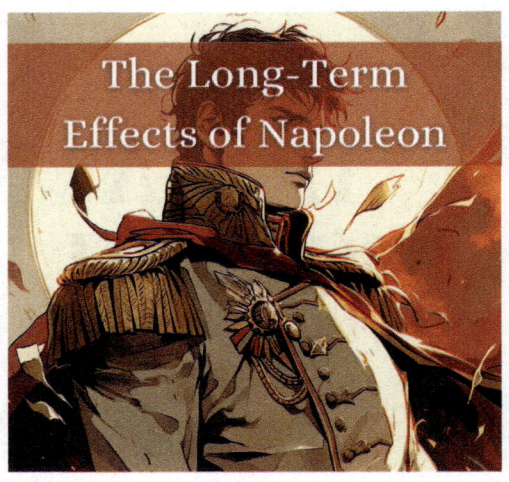

Greetings, dear reader, as we approach the end of our long journey through the life of Napoleon Bonaparte, it's time to consider his lasting impact. This chapter focuses on the long-term effects of Napoleon's rule in France and across Europe.

Reformation in France

After the chaos of the French Revolution, Napoleon brought much-needed stability to France. His legal reform, the Napoleonic Code, remains one of his most enduring legacies. It established clear laws around property, family, and individual rights, replacing the patchwork of laws that had existed in different regions of France before the Revolution. To this day, the Napoleonic Code forms the basis of civil law in many countries around the world.

Napoleon's impact was not limited to the legal sphere. He championed education, especially in science and mathematics, leading to the establishment of various lycees, or secondary schools, and the famous French institution, the Polytechnique. Napoleon also modernized financial and administrative systems, setting up the Bank of France and introducing the efficient "prefect" system for local administration.

Effects on Europe

Beyond France, Napoleon's influence was felt across Europe. He dismantled the Holy Roman Empire, reorganizing it into the more streamlined Confederation of the Rhine. This eventually paved the way for German unification in the late 19th century.

His ambitious military campaigns spread the ideas of the French Revolution – liberty, equality, and fraternity – far and wide. His advances brought about the end of feudalism in many parts of Europe and spread the influence of French culture, politics, and law.

Downfall and Continuation of Influence

While Napoleon's ambition eventually led to his downfall, it also brought about a new balance of power in Europe. After his defeat at Waterloo, the Congress of Vienna in 1815 redrew the map of Europe in an attempt to maintain a delicate equilibrium among the continent's major powers. This balance helped maintain relative peace in Europe for nearly a century, until the outbreak of World War I.

Despite his exile and death, Napoleon's influence continued to be felt across the globe. His nephew, Napoleon III, would even become Emperor of France decades later, ruling during a period known as the Second French Empire.

A Man of Paradoxes

Napoleon was a man of paradoxes, a fact that contributes to his enduring fascination. A champion of the French Revolution who crowned himself Emperor, a reformer who built an empire on the backs of countless soldiers, a military genius who met with an ignominious end - these contradictions make him a fascinating figure, even more than two centuries after his death.

As we conclude this chapter, we're reminded that Napoleon Bonaparte was a man who embodied the drama and contradictions of his age. His life is a testament to both the possibilities and dangers of unchecked ambition. His legacy, complicated as it may be, has undeniably shaped the world we live in today.

In the next, and final, chapter of our journey, we'll reflect on Napoleon's life, ambition, genius, and downfall. We'll consider how a man from a minor nobility on a small Mediterranean island rose to become one of the most powerful figures in world history, only to lose it all. It's been quite the journey, hasn't it, dear reader? Let's finish it together.

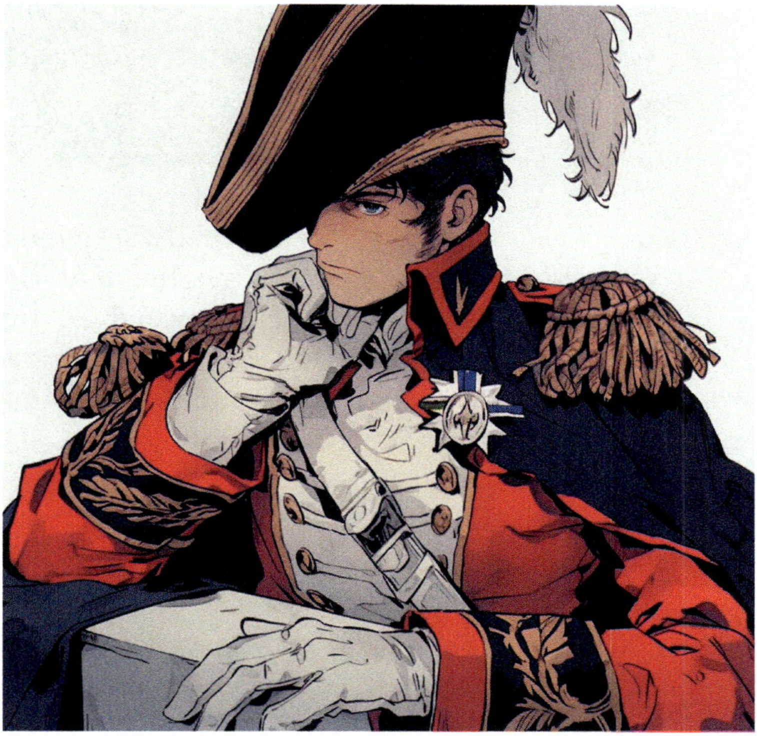

Chapter 27: Napoleon Shaped the Course of World

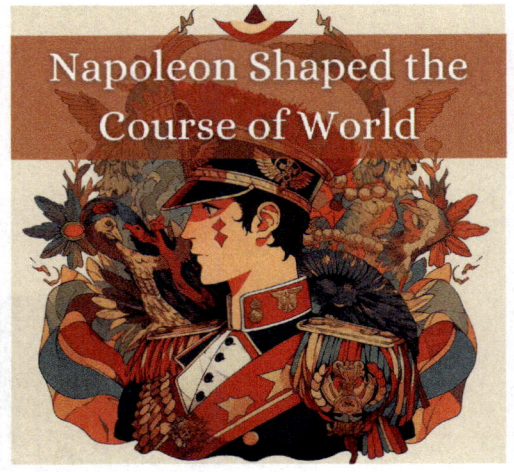

Greetings again, dear reader! We've reached the penultimate chapter of our epic journey through the life and times of Napoleon Bonaparte. The previous chapter delved into the direct effects of Napoleon's reign on France and Europe. Now, let's broaden our perspective to understand how Napoleon's actions, ideals, and even his mistakes significantly influenced the course of world history.

Spreading Revolutionary Ideals

The French Revolution, with its novel concepts of liberty, equality, and fraternity, sent shockwaves throughout Europe. Napoleon, coming to power in the aftermath, became a key carrier of these ideas. Through his military campaigns, he dismantled the vestiges of feudalism and introduced civil liberties in many parts of Europe. While his primary aim was domination rather than liberation, the revolutionary ideals often left a lasting impact, stirring up demands for greater democracy and national self-determination.

Remapping Europe

Napoleon redrew the boundaries of Europe, both physically and metaphorically. He dissolved the Holy Roman Empire, paving the way for the emergence of a united Germany in the late 19th century. His Napoleonic Code, with its emphasis on equality before the law and protection of civil liberties, became a benchmark for legal systems around the world.

Influencing Modern Military Strategy

From a military perspective, Napoleon is often seen as a pioneer of modern warfare. His tactics and strategies, including the Corps system, emphasis on speed and mobility, and the use of mass conscription, influenced many later military leaders. Indeed, his principles of war are still taught in military academies around the globe today.

Setting Precedents in International Relations

Following Napoleon's defeat, the Congress of Vienna in 1815 set new precedents for international relations. It established a balance of power that, while flawed, aimed to prevent a single nation from dominating Europe, thus anticipating some principles of today's international diplomacy. The post-Napoleonic era also saw the emergence of nationalism as a powerful political force, a development that would shape the history of the following centuries.

An Enduring Icon

Napoleon Bonaparte has become an enduring icon, immortalized in countless books, paintings, and even movies. He is a figure who continues to fascinate, serving as a potent symbol of ambition, genius, but also the perils of hubris.

Conclusion

Our journey with Napoleon has traversed the highs of his power and the lows of his downfall, exploring along the way how his influence reverberated across continents and ages. It's clear that the Corsican upstart who became a French emperor shaped the course of world history in profound ways.

As we prepare to delve into the final chapter, we will reflect on the totality of Napoleon's life, considering the interplay of his ambition, genius, and downfall, and the indelible legacy that this complex man left behind. Let's draw this fascinating narrative to its close together, dear reader, for every story, no matter how grand, must have its ending.

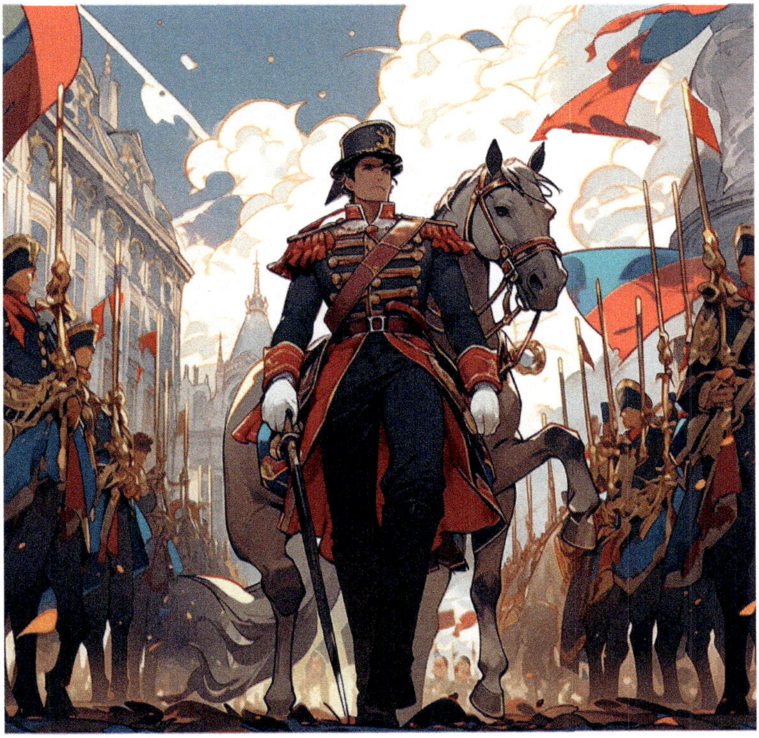

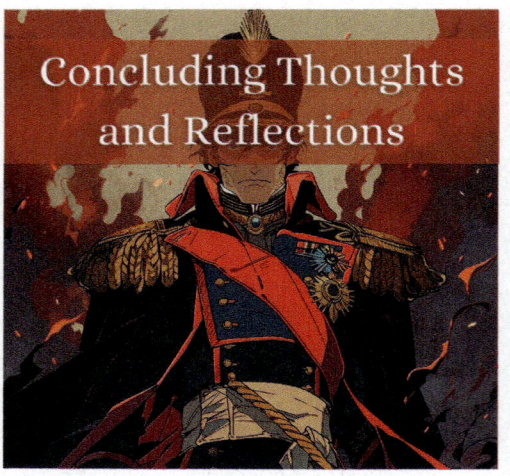

Chapter 28: Concluding Thoughts and Reflections

Well, my dear reader, we've made it. From the cobblestone streets of Ajaccio, Corsica to the remote and windswept island of Saint Helena, we have followed in the footsteps of Napoleon Bonaparte. As we cross the finish line of this epic narrative journey, it's time to reflect on the man who was Napoleon, on his breathtaking ambition, his undeniable genius, and ultimately, his tragic downfall.

Ambition and Ascension

Napoleon was a man marked by extraordinary ambition, an attribute that served as a double-edged sword. It was his burning desire to make a name for himself that propelled him out of his obscure birthplace and onto the global stage. He reshaped France and Europe according to his own grand vision, marking an era with his name.

But ambition, when left unchecked, can often overreach. Napoleon's desire for supremacy blinded him to the complexities of nation-building and to the resilience of those who resisted him. His hunger for control, for territory, for legacy, set him on a collision course with the wider forces of history.

The Genius of Napoleon

Yet, we must not forget the genius of Napoleon, which shone in both the military and civil arenas. He revolutionized warfare with his strategies, reformed the French legal system, and left a lasting impact on administrative structures that extended well beyond his reign.

The Downfall

However, even a genius can stumble and fall. Napoleon's downfall lay, paradoxically, in his strengths. His military boldness led him to the frozen disaster of Russia. His firm belief in his destiny made him deaf to the advice of his counselors. His ambition led him to underestimate his European adversaries, ultimately uniting them against him. His self-constructed image as a modern Caesar led to overreach and defeat.

Legacy

Despite his tragic end, Napoleon's impact on the world did not fade away. From the laws we abide by, to the boundaries of nations, to the very ideas of what constitutes modern leadership, we are still living in the shadows of his Grande Armée.

Conclusion

Our journey through Napoleon's life story has been a voyage across the peaks and valleys of human potential. It has shown us how an individual, armed with ambition, intelligence, and an unwavering belief in himself, can shape the course of history. Yet, it has also shown us the perils of hubris and the inevitability of fall when ambition oversteps its bounds.

As we conclude this narrative, I encourage you, dear reader, to reflect on the layers and contradictions of this complex historical figure. For, in understanding Napoleon, we gain insights not only into history but also into the intricate weave of human character, and the profound forces that drive us towards greatness or ruin.

Thank you for joining me on this journey. I hope our exploration of Napoleon Bonaparte has not only educated but also inspired and provoked thought, for that is the ultimate goal of engaging with history. Until our next historical adventure, I bid you adieu.

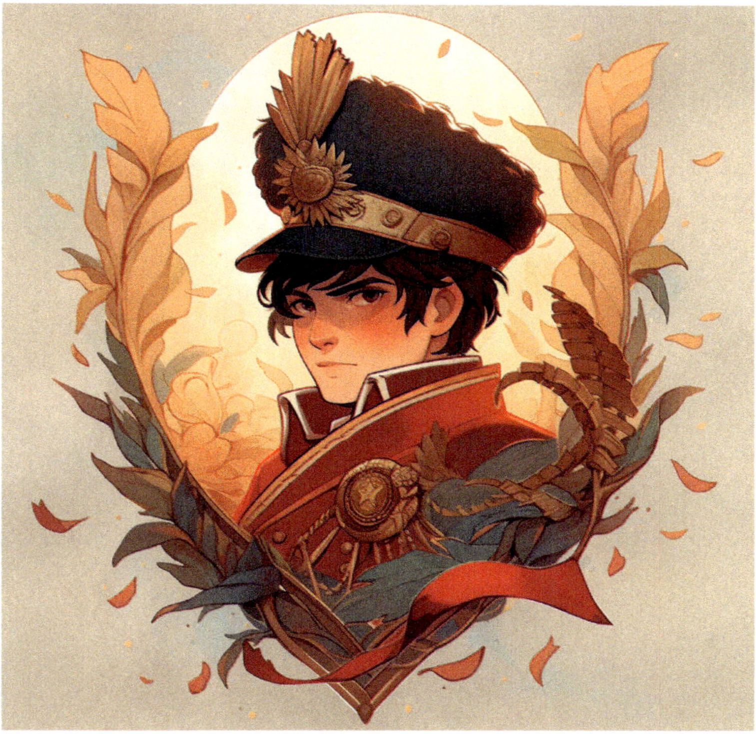

Printed in Great Britain
by Amazon